Good for a Laugh

Good for

by

BENNETT CERF

a Laugh

a new collection of
humorous tidbits and anecdotes from
AARDVARK to ZYTHUM

with illustrations by **DOUG ANDERSON**

HANOVER HOUSE, Garden City, New York

Foreword

Motion picture producers have discovered that Somerset Maugham's shrewd, crisp, and superbly told short stories are stuff from which sure-fire screen fare can be fashioned. To introduce the last sheaf they even persuaded him to face the camera personally and say a few words. He contented himself by pointing out that although his stories were founded on fact, they emerged as fiction. "Like every other author," he added, "I have looked upon it as my right to arrange my facts to suit my purpose, which was to entertain."

Mr. Maugham put the words right into my mouth. The stories in this collection—like the five others that preceded it—are, for the most part, not new, but I have retold them in my own fashion, adding a detail here and there to heighten an effect, changing the setting, props, or even the cast of characters when occasion seemed to warrant. *Good for a Laugh* is not history. It is meant for amusement. If in some cases I failed to credit the actual source of a story, I at least did my best to note who told it to *me*. Arthur Brisbane once quoted his rival editor, Herbert Bayard Swope, in a Sunday article. Swope phoned promptly to say, "I remember telling you that story, Arthur, but I believe it was first attributed to Count Metternich." "Swope," said Brisbane, "I always pin a story to the last man who told it to me, and you're the first man I've credited with a good one who ever objected!"

Many of the stories in this book are reprinted, with permission, from my "Cerf Board" column in *This Week Magazine*, "Trade Winds" in the *Saturday Review*, and my daily stint, "Try and Stop Me" for the King Features Syndicate. Because many after-dinner speakers, club officers, and members of the clergy and bar have complained that they experienced difficulty in my previous collection in finding just the story that would fill some need of their own, I've made an effort to arrange this volume for easier reference. I hope you will like it that way. I'd appreciate your letting me know. It's always pleasant to hear from readers—even if all they have to say is that their great-grandfather told the story on page 67 a heck of a lot better than I did.

There is nothing like a good, hearty laugh to relieve a tense situation, or soothe nerves that have been stretched too tight. I've always preferred hearing a funny story to being told just why it made me chuckle. I remember with a shudder the learned party who covered over three hundred pages some years ago explaining what caused people to laugh. Wolcott Gibbs inspected the result with dismay that topped mine. His exact comment—and heaven grant that he never says it about me!—was, "Mr. So-and-so has got humor down—and is breaking its arm."

BENNETT CERF

Mount Kisco, New York
September, 1952

Contents

Good for a Laugh

A is for our
ARMED FORCES

It stood to reason that the current remobilization program would cause a revival of all the time-honored military gags that served so well in the two World Wars—and were already fully matured, in many cases, even earlier than that. Back into circulation have come the stories of the tough sergeant who caught a rookie with a single button of his blouse unfastened, and roared, "Sun-bathing, eh?"; the billy-goat who chewed up a congressional report and enthused, "Best darn propaganda I ever ate"; and the mermaid who bobbed up alongside a destroyer with an infant in her arms and asked a gob on deck, "Do you happen to know whether there's an Ensign Floyd attached to this ship?" And the day before this volume went to press, a TV comic revived the old favorite about the dear lass who cabled her sweetheart in Korea, "Couldn't wait another day for you, darling, so married your father. Love, Mother."

A detachment of Marines, sent to the rear after valiant service in the front lines, was engaged in the usual evening bull session, and the subject, as usual, got around to the girls who had been left behind. Were they faithful, or were they not?

The one who had the least doubt was a blond-haired young

11

corporal from Hoboken. "My girl's not doing any playing around," he announced with absolute conviction. "How can you be so sure?" asked a friend.

"Well, for one thing," said the corporal, "she's got three more years to serve in reform school."

A veteran of the Korean fighting, now in officer-candidate school, likes to tell about the day he was inducted into the Army. His physical over, he was taken in hand by a sergeant and asked, "Did you go to grammar school?"

"Yes, sir," said the draftee. "I also went through high school, graduated cum laude from college, completed three years of graduate studies at Cornell, and then acquired two more degrees at Columbia."

The sergeant nodded, reached for a rubber stamp, and slapped it on the questionnaire. It consisted of a single word: "Literate."

In the early days of World War II, wild rumors about invading Jap planes being sighted within range of the California coast swept the panicky denizens of Hollywood. One of the highest moguls of MGM took them so seriously that he summoned the most famous camouflage expert in the United States and told him, "I want the entire MGM studio camouflaged immediately, regardless of cost." "I'm sorry," said the expert, "but I can't take the job." The mogul, who hadn't heard the word "no" in twenty years, was aghast. "What do you mean you can't?" he sputtered. "This is rank discrimination against the motion-picture industry! I'll have you run out of the state." "Calm yourself," advised the expert. "If you will stop shouting long enough I'll explain why I can't take the job. The Army has ordered that for every essential plant we camouflage an alternate target has to be set up. And you might as well know that MGM has been designated the alternate target for Douglas Aircraft." The mogul was revived an hour or so later.

During the Nazi occupation of Paris, a burly, mean-looking storm trooper strode into a subway car and tripped headlong over the umbrella of a meek little old lady who sat near the door. He picked himself up, bruised and besmirched, and launched into a tirade of abuse against the terrified old lady. Then, suddenly conscious of the hostile glares of the other occupants of the car, he lurched out at the next station. The passengers waited until he was gone, then burst into spontaneous applause for the little woman with the umbrella. She hung her head modestly and said, "I know it isn't much—but he's the fifth one I bagged today."

Quentin Reynolds tells about the Englishman, Arabian and Yank who were conversing on a street corner in Casablanca when a spectacular Oriental beauty ankled by. The Englishman exclaimed, "By Jove!" The Arabian murmured a reverent, "By Allah!" The Yank breathed softly, "By tomorrow night!"

When Cecil Brown was reporting the early days of World War II in Mussolini's Rome, he became convinced that his regular waiter was spying on him, and demanded that he be fired forthwith. "But I cannot do that," expostulated the hotel manager. "How do I know whether the next spy will be such an efficient waiter?"

John Straley met a veteran pilot of World War II who was afraid that he couldn't begin to handle the 1952 model, because of all the new gadgets and refinements that had been installed. "I took one test," he confessed. "The elementary stuff was a cinch, but then the fellow who was asking questions demanded, 'Suppose you were at an altitude of 20,000 feet, going 650 miles an hour. Suddenly your oxygen tank breaks loose, one motor catches fire, and a wing crumples. You have no parachute. What do you do?'" Mr. Straley asked, "What did you answer?" "I didn't answer," confessed the former pilot. "From the question alone, I blacked out."

In Seattle, they've revived the story about the destroyer on a trial run whose captain suddenly noticed that the ship was zig-zagging all over the Pacific. Charging to the bridge, he found a white-faced ensign at the helm, and roared, "Man alive, do you realize we're fully forty degrees off our course?" "Sorry, sir," mumbled the ensign (just graduated from a quickie course at a Midwestern naval station), "but you see, I never drove one of these things before!"

All the way back to Civil War days can be traced the yarn about a captain who was offered a bribe to carry some contraband through the Northern blockade. "It's worth $250 to me," whispered the smuggler. "No," said the captain firmly. "I'm a man of honor." The smuggler raised his offer to $500, then $750, but the captain still turned a deaf ear. Finally the smuggler said, "I'll give you $1000." The captain drew a gun and shouted, "Off my ship, you varmint! You're getting too close to my price."

Sign spotted by Harold Helfer on a bulletin board of an army airport in Indiana: "Notice! Absolutely no flying permitted over nudist camp exactly eight miles SSW on a true course of 190 degrees."

Two effeminate-looking young men appeared to be inseparable for months, but suddenly one of them was drafted, and the other mournfully turned up at one of their old haunts alone. "Where's your pal?" asked the bartender. "Oh, my dear," was the excited reply, "haven't you heard? He's fighting for Aunt Sam!"

A Kentucky doctor, testing a hill boy's mental capacities for the local draft board, asked, "What would you say is the difference between a little boy and a dwarf?" "Might be a heap of difference," allowed the hill boy. "Such as?" encouraged the doctor. The prospective infantryman drawled, "That dwarf might be a girl."

A gawky new draftee from Tennessee suddenly recognized a fellow townsman across the parade field. The fact that the fellow townsman was sporting a first lieutenant's uniform didn't bother him for a second. He strolled over, whacked the officer on the back, and drawled, "Good to see you again, Joe, old fellah. How goes it?" The lieutenant flushed with anger (fully a hundred other soldiers had enjoyed the incident) and told the draftee off in a three-minute oration that left nothing to anybody's imagination. When he finally ran out of breath, the draftee, utterly unabashed, exclaimed, "Lawdy, Joe. If I'd a-knowed you was going to carry on like that, I'd never a-spoke to you at all."

A young man in Tallahassee claimed exemption on the grounds of defective eyesight. He brought his wife along as evidence.

A tight-lipped general, obviously a martinet, descended upon a draftee camp in New England on an inspection tour, and a regimental parade was arranged in his honor. As the band marched by the reviewing stand, the general emitted a snort of disgust and roared, "Halt!" Three battalions stopped in their tracks. "Now back up," hollered the general, "and the next time that band marches past me I want to see the slides of those trombones going in and out together!"

When I was taken for a ride in a new jet plane at Eglin Field, Florida, recently, the pilot didn't make me any happier by explaining, "If we have to bail out, just press this red button. You and the seat will go sailing out together. Then count ten and pull this strap." Fortunately this program, which struck me as somewhat drastic, never had to be executed. Back on terra firma, the pilot explained that you couldn't parachute out of a jet plane in the old way because you were going too darn fast; the rush of air would do you in before the parachute could be opened. One pilot, he added, had to abandon his craft in Korea. He managed to wriggle free of the seat and other encumbrances and landed reasonably intact back of the U.N. lines where a rescue crew picked him up. "Feel O.K.?" he was asked. "Well," he answered, "I guess you guys have heard of flotsam and jetsam. I'm the jetsam."

Bob Hope was having a tight golf match in Los Angeles one morning with the kingpin of the U. S. Air Force, General Hoyt Vandenburg, when a formation of jet planes whooshed above the course. Hope loudly instructed his caddy, "Better tell those lads to feather their engines. Their boss is trying to sink a twelve-foot putt!"

In an airborne recruit squadron learning the technique of parachute jumping, there was one lad who stuttered very badly. When his group made its first jump the instructions were, "Count ten, then pull the handle that releases your parachute." The stutterer's companions were floating gently to the ground when he plummeted by, his parachute unopened. "The poor bastard," mourned his pal, "I knew he'd never have time to count to ten."

A big dance hall, located across the way from a National Guard encampment in New England, enticed trade from the men in uniform with this sign: "Come and dance with our 50 beautiful hostesses—50. Generals: $10.00. Colonels: $8.00. Captains and Lieutenants: $6.00. Enlisted men: $3.00. Veterans of World War I: 25 cents an hour."

A is for
AUTOMOBILES

The officially stated reasons for most divorces in the United States are infidelity, incompatibility, or non-support, but the rock on which thousands of these marital craft first begin to founder is undoubtedly women's unerring ability to get lost on the shortest and simplest of automobile journeys. The Lord gave women any number of alluring curves and protuberances, but unfortunately, a good bump of direction was not included among them.

I began pursuing this line of thought when I heard my wife on the phone one day telling Nedda (Mrs. Josh) Logan how to negotiate the dozen odd miles between her home in Connecticut and ours in Mount Kisco. "You can't miss the way," said my Phyllis cheerfully. "Just take Route 104—or is it 105?—till you hit Number 22 at Bedford, then swing left—or right—and you'll find yourself at a junction with 172—or maybe it's 182. At any rate, just cross the railroad tracks and go up a steep hill and you'll see a sign marked 'Cerf.' That's us." These instructions seemed a trifle ambiguous to me but they evidently didn't bother Mrs. Logan, for the girls were discussing animatedly what they were going to wear by the time I had staggered to the telephone. Needless to say, our dinner party was held up indefinitely by the non-arrival of Mrs. Logan. Some two hours after she had been scheduled to appear, she phoned to announce, "What do I do now? I seem to be in Buffalo."

Mrs. Logan did get to Mount Kisco in time for a midnight snack, but when the hour came for her to return home, she loftily declined my offer to draw her a small map. "I'll just go back the way I came," she announced confidently. Next day, however, I learned inadvertently that she had driven fifteen miles past her own entrance way. "How did you know you had gone too far?" I asked. She looked at me pityingly and snapped, "I guess I know the Stamford railroad station when I see it."

The real marital imbroglios on the open road occurred before our highways were numbered and marked, and tourists had to depend for directions on detailed routes in automobile blue books. The husband would crank up the old Maxwell or Winton, the wife would spread open the blue book on her lap, and off they would tootle, "jogging left at 31.8 with trolley tracks," "turning sharp right at 46.7 at statue of Ebeneazer Twuffle," or "avoiding steep-graded macadam turn-off at 58.3." Unfortunately, friend wife almost invariably forgot to mention one imperative turn somewhere along the line, and the happy couple would suddenly find themselves at a dead end in Princeton, instead of Mrs. Wimpfheimer's country seat in Asbury Park. Then the recriminations started and continued far into the night, with the husband usually concluding, "Until you learn how to read a simple printed page, I suggest we make our future journeys by rail."

Aunt Emma grew somewhat eccentric in her declining years, but since the whole family hoped to inherit some of her considerable fortune, she was humored in every impulse. One afternoon, at the height of a furious storm, Aunt Emma decided she'd like a ride in the family convertible, with the top down. Uncle Herbert dutifully escorted her to the car, climbed behind the wheel, and without ever budging from the garage, went through the motions of taking her for a drive. At the end of a half hour Aunt Emma

pronounced herself satisfied, and the two of them re-entered the living room. "Herbert is a fair enough driver," admitted Aunt Emma, "but I think he's just a little bit off his rocker. Here we were driving through a raging downpour, with the top down, and the darn fool never put on his hat!"

Two silver-haired old ladies wobbled down the main street of a New England town in their moth-eaten coupé, made an illegal turn, and compounded their felony by ignoring the outraged traffic officer's endeavors to stop them. He finally caught up with them in front of Ye Olde Waffle Shoppe. "Didn't you hear my whistle?" he demanded angrily. The perky octogenarian at the wheel looked at him coyly and admitted, "Yes, I did, officer—but I never flirt when I'm driving." The cop looked astonished, then broke into a broad grin, and said, "You win, lady! Drive on!"

Driving through a blinding rainstorm, Mr. Wheedle was further harassed by the incessant nagging and criticism of his wife beside him. Suddenly, however, she ceased talking, and simply sat there shaking her head back and forth vigorously. Mr. Wheedle enjoyed the respite without question for about twenty miles, but then decided to investigate the phenomenon. He soon discovered what had happened. Mrs. Wheedle's nose was firmly caught in the windshield wiper!

"A pessimist," explained Grover Whalen at a recent dinner for traffic regulators, "is a female who's afraid she won't be able to squeeze her car into a very small parking space. An optimist is a male who thinks she won't try." Lee Gillespie, of Council Bluffs, writes, "I've discovered how to get rid of a noise in your car. Let *her* drive." Allan McMahon, the Fort Wayne capitalist, says you can always pick out the owner of a car in which six ladies are riding. She's the one who, after somebody pulls the door shut, always opens it and slams it harder.

A chap named Williams and his wife journeyed from their home in Jackson Heights to visit an author in Pennsylvania. Mrs. Williams had a map spread out on her lap and suddenly exclaimed, "Slow up! You turn right on this road here." Williams turned right, but grumbled, "I don't like the looks of this road." He liked it even less when it tailed off into a cowpath through a thick wood. Stopping the car, he cried, "Let me look at that map." Aggrieved, Mrs. Williams protested, "You never will trust me. Here's the road on the map, just as I said it was." Mr. Williams investigated, closed his eyes wearily, and explained, "Darling, that is not a road. That is the state border line."

John Kimberley, of Minneapolis, celebrated his birthday recently with a gay party at which Mrs. Kimberley made a slight error. She drank a full glass of gasoline, happily convinced that it was straight imported gin. When the party broke up, recalls the host, all the other revelers were hiccuping. Poor Mrs. Kimberley, however, was honking.

A railroad claim agent was teaching his wife to drive, when the brakes suddenly failed on a steep downhill grade. "I can't stop," she shrilled. "What'll I do?" "Brace yourself," advised her husband, "and try to hit something cheap."

Mr. Young checked his monthly garage bill with growing ire, and complained to his wife, "Why, the robber charged me $20 to tow you a mile to the service station that day you got stuck on Ninetieth Street." "That's not exorbitant," maintained Mrs. Young. "He earned every penny of it. I had the brakes jammed on all the way."

What Henry Mencken would call a typical female motorist came tootling merrily down the wrong side of a crowded thoroughfare and ran smack into Mr. Jordan's brand-new convertible. While they were trying to untangle bumpers, the lady driver said grudgingly, "I'm afraid this was largely my fault." "Nonsense," said Mr. Jordan with a gallant bow. "I assure you the blame rests entirely with me. I saw you fully three blocks away and had ample time to dart down a side street."

B is for
BROADWAY

Sir Laurence Olivier, who returned in triumph to Broadway to co-star with his beautiful wife, Vivien Leigh, in Shakespeare's *Antony and Cleopatra* and Shaw's *Caesar and Cleopatra* (the dual bill was referred to by the trade as *Two on the Nile*), is one of the most charming and versatile actors alive. He's equally at home in stark tragedy, drawing-room comedy, or knockabout clowning in a benefit performance with Danny Kaye.

He learned his profession the hard way, touring the hinterlands of Britain and Wales with an obscure troupe, playing in houses so ill-equipped that most changes had to be made in public washrooms. Olivier still refers to those days as his "tour with the lavatory theatre." His fame in America dates back to the time Samuel Goldwyn persuaded him to play the lead in the memorable screen version of *Wuthering Heights*.

The picture was released in 1939—a banner year for the Oliviers, because it also marked Miss Leigh's triumph in *Gone with the Wind*.

Gone with the Wind having been written in Atlanta by a native daughter, Margaret Mitchell, it was fitting that the world première of the picture be given there. The hysterical hoop-la that attended the event gave ample indication that this celluloid epic of the Civil War was destined to be the biggest grossing picture in the history of Hollywood. Receipts now top the thirty-million mark, with the end nowhere in sight. The sum is greater than the total assessed value of all the Atlanta real estate and property actually burned down by General Sherman's order on that disastrous November day in 1864. People go to see the picture again and again. One English visitor was astounded recently by the skyscrapers and welter of traffic around the Five Points in Downtown Atlanta. "I'd seen Atlanta burned down so often in *Gone with the Wind*," he confessed, "that I was rather bowled over to find any of it standing at all."

The Five Points on that opening night in December, 1939, was a sight to behold. Governor Rivers had proclaimed a stateside holiday, urged the womenfolk to don hoop skirts and pantalets, and appealed to the males to sprout sideburns and goatees and try to look as much like Clark Gable as possible. They complied with a will—and also practically tore off Gable's uniform when he appeared in person. Georgia's immortal athlete, golfer Bobby Jones, and baseball's one and only Tyrus Raymond Cobb, were invited, along with the governors of five neighboring states. Only the authoress, Miss Mitchell, failed to appear.

Miss Leigh, possibly due to the influence of a well-known soft-drink company located in Atlanta, acknowledged the wild plaudits of the multitude with, "Ah, this is the applause that refreshes!" And an eleven-year-old girl, given her choice of a Christmas bicycle or meeting Clark Gable, unhesitatingly chose Gable. When he kissed her, she closed her eyes in ecstasy and exclaimed, "Now I am a woman!"

Gertrude Lawrence was starring in a London play that was honored by a visit from the late King and his Queen. As Queen Elizabeth entered the Royal Box, the entire audience arose to acclaim her. Miss Lawrence, watching from the wings, murmured, "What an entrance!" Noel Coward, on tiptoe behind her, added, "What a part!"

Deems Taylor tells a story to show that even the greatest get twinges of jealousy. He attended an audition of young talent with Alfred Lunt and Lynn Fontanne. The participants—mostly female—quavered their way through the sleepwalking scene in *Macbeth*.

Afterward, Lynn whispered to Taylor, "Absolutely no talent in the whole group," and added, "thank God!"

Carl Sandburg was persuaded to attend the dress rehearsal of a very serious play by a very serious young dramatist, but unfortunately slept through a greater part of the performance. The outraged dramatist chided him later, "How could you sleep when you knew how much I wanted your opinion?" Sandburg reminded him, "Young man, sleep *is* an opinion."

Veteran stage producer Max Gordon warns all aspiring new playwrights, "The curtain goes up and two people are out on the stage, and somebody better say something pretty damn fast."

London society blinked at the frankness of a former musical comedy star who married an earl and, when asked by a sob sister, "How does it feel to marry into royalty?" exulted, "Ah, the peace and tranquillity of the double bed after the hurly-burly of the chaise longue!"

Somerset Maugham gravely informed the students in a drama course at London University: "A sure formula for success is to write first a tragedy in five acts. Put it away in a drawer for six months, then change it into a comedy in three acts. Forget it for another year. Then reduce it to a curtain raiser. That done, rush right out and marry a rich American."

High among the countless anecdotes about the stuttering comedian, Joe Frisco, ranks the one about the time Joe was regaling his friends with a yarn when a midget walked over unobserved, propped his chin on the edge of the table, and regarded Joe with a melancholy stare. Joe took one look, gulped convulsively, and screamed to the waiter, "W-w-what's the idea? I didn't order J-j-john the Baptist!"

Howard Lindsay, now engaged with Russel Crouse on their tenth collaboration—as happy and successful a relationship as the theatre has ever known—is punctilious about his business engagements but on the forgetful side when it comes to social functions. He has been known to wander off from one of his own dinner parties for a brief nap and then forget to come downstairs again. Names of friends and acquaintances frequently elude him. When in doubt he calls everybody Herb, except his friend Herb Mayes, whom he hails as Jerry. For years he engaged in a bitter feud with an actor who had let him down and wouldn't even stay in the same room with him when they accidentally met at a party. Then one night Lindsay's wife, Dorothy Stickney, was amazed to find him in close and harmonious conversation with the actor at the other end of a Hollywood drawing room. The conference ended in a burst of laughter, and Lindsay clapped the actor on the back. "I wonder what caused Howard to forgive him?" thought Mrs. Lindsay. At this moment, Lindsay whispered hoarsely in her ear, "Who *was* that fellow I just was talking to, anyhow?"

Mrs. Howard Lindsay remembers with some qualms the special performance of *Life with Father* she and her distinguished spouse staged for Franklin D. Roosevelt in Washington. She was so terrified before the curtain rose that she was heard to murmur, "I wouldn't do this again for the President of the United States!" Later at an after-theatre dinner in the White House a member of the troupe was even more nervous than Miss Stickney. She quavered to the President, "What an imposing building the White House is! Do you happen to recall the name of the artichoke who designed it?"

Monty Woolley slipped on the stairs of the Times Square subway station one rainy night when there were no taxis to be had. Halfway down, he bumped into a stout lady, who toppled against him, and landed in his lap at the bottom of the stairs. Woolley tapped her on the shoulder and pointed out, "Madam, I'm sorry, but this is as far as I go."

An actress who had received a magnificent diamond necklace as a gift from "Diamond Jim" Brady hit upon what she thought was an excellent device for safeguarding it. She simply left it openly on her dressing table when she went out, with a note nearby reading, "This is just an imitation. The original is in my safe-deposit box." One night, however, she returned to find the necklace gone. In its place was this penciled message, "Thanks, lady. The substitute is just what I wanted. I'm a substitute myself. The burglar who usually covers this hotel is away on vacation."

A persistent playwright forced the same manuscript on the late producing wizard, David Belasco, seven times, always claiming that important revisions had made it the stuff from which sure hits were fashioned. "It's awful," Belasco said finally. "All the great playwrights combined couldn't doctor it sufficiently." "Isn't there some way you can put it on the stage?" persisted the playwright. "Yes," snapped Belasco, his patience exhausted. "Give me the script." He tossed it to his assistant and ordered, "Chop this up and use it as the snowstorm tonight."

A luscious chorus girl sued a rich playboy for breach of promise and was awarded the round sum of $25,000 by a sympathetic jury. Emerging from the courthouse in an understandably happy daze, she was promptly run into by a truck and couldn't sit down for four weeks. For this mishap, however, she collected only two hundred dollars' damages in court. The moral of this sad story is clear: Never trifle with a fair maid's heart: kick her in the pants!

There's a strip-tease making the rounds who has trained a flock of doves to divest her of as many of her seven veils as local gendarmes will allow. One evening, one of the doves got bored with its job, fluttered across the footlights and settled on the shoulder of a surprised spectator. The house manager observed, "I've been in show business twenty years—and that's the first time I ever saw an actress give the audience the bird."

In their history of the past fifty years in the theatre, *Show Biz*, Abel Green and Joe Laurie, Jr., chronicle the first public appearance of Mae West. The now-famous interpreter of the lush role of "Diamond Lil" made her debut at the Model Theatre in Philadelphia in 1912. Her billing read, "Watch her do a muscle dance sitting down—and her movement is all her own." By the time Miss West reached New Haven, the Yale boys were trying to tear down the house—and not from rage. The local critic observed, "Miss West wore a trick dress with a catch that seemed to break very easily, thereby delivering the full value of her personality."

A young lady from the Bronx landed a job in a big Broadway night club and by way of celebration brought home a small bottle of champagne to share with her family. She had barely popped the cork when her mother ran to the telephone and called the doctor. "You should come quick," ordered mama. "Sadie's got us drinking shampoo!"

Eddie Foy, Jr., tells about the chorus girl's daughter who attended public school for the first time. The teacher asked her, "What does Y-E-S spell?" The little girl answered, "Mink."

There's a featured aerialist in this year's big circus troupe who always misses his big trick a couple of times on purpose to emphasize its difficulty. Then, while the drums roll and audiences gasp, he does it to perfection. One night, however, he told the manager, "If you don't mind, I'm going to do my climactic trick right the first time tonight. I'm tired."

News flashes from the circus: A trapeze artist married the In-
dia-rubber man, and is now twisting him around her little finger.
The lion tamer is angry at his lady friend because, he says, she
kisses him and gives him a brush-off at the same time. Seems she's
the bearded lady. And the assistant manager has tried tonics of
eleven different colors to cure his dandruff. He reports, "I finally
got rid of the dandruff, all right, but now my head is full of con-
fetti."

When the rodeo was packing them in at Madison Square Garden, an elderly lady paused after the show for a cup of java in a
beanery down the block. The coffee was too hot for her and she
put it down with a sigh, exclaiming, "Oh, dear, my bus leaves in
three minutes." A polite cowboy promptly handed his cup to her,
explaining, "Lady, I'll be obliged if you drink this coffee of mine.
It's already saucered and blowed."

A magician seeking booking at Radio City Music Hall asserted,
"I've got a new trick that will panic them." "What is it?" asked the
manager. "I saw a woman in half," announced the magician. "Call
that a new trick?" scoffed the manager. "They've been doing that
around here for years." "Oh, yeah?" countered the magician.
"Lengthwise?"

Another unique stage attraction is a lady who has trained her
dog to curl itself around her neck and remain absolutely motion-
less there—a perfect imitation of a fur neckpiece. "I taught my
dog the trick for a special reason," she explained. "Lots of hotels

are silly enough to keep dogs out entirely. Now that my Fido can look so much like a fur piece, I can smuggle him into all the hotels on earth." "And how," asked Mr. George S. Kaufman acidly, "do you get in yourself?"

"When I was a kid living in a tenement," says Eddie Cantor, "we didn't know what an elevator was. It was a six-story climb to our little apartment. When I got the sniffles, Mama would yell out of the window to the doctor, 'What should I give Eddie?' and he'd yell back, 'Give him a dose of castor oil and throw down a dollar.'"

Comedian Joe E. Brown, famous for the generous proportions of his buccal cavity, was dining at the home of a Broadway producer. The hostess urged him to try the new recipe for strawberry short cake. "Gotta watch my figure, but I'll try just a mouthful," compromised Joe. "That's fine," said the hostess. "Maggie, fill up the gentleman's plate."

Mrs. Gabor and her three talented and beautiful daughters, Eva, Zsa Zsa and Magda, attract publicity and men with equal facility. Recently one gentleman caller expressed a need for food to help him cope with the girls.

"Raid the icebox," suggested Mama Gabor. "It's always full of good things to eat." The visitor found that the entire contents of the icebox consisted of two dozen orchids and a salami.

The first time Martha Raye ate at the famous Pump Room in Chicago, she was a member of a dinner party hosted by Jimmy Durante. When a waiter passed with a portion of shishkebab (lamb on a flaming sword—a specialty of the house), Miss Raye was startled and exclaimed, "What on earth was that?" Durante explained, "A customer who only left a ten-dollar tip."

Novelist Robert Sylvester has a young friend who is an ardent devotee of bebop music. The wilder and more discordant it waxes, the better he likes it. He was walking his best girl home very late one night when a garbage van pulled up ahead and the crew began banging and rattling cans of refuse about the sidewalk in that copyrighted manner best calculated to wake up everybody on the block. At the height of the racket the bebop devotee clasped his girl's hand and murmured reverently, "Listen, darling! Our song!"

B is for
BARBERS

The fixtures and equipment of a big barber shop in a metropolitan hotel are a lot flossier than those of a tonsorial parlor in a small town, but the atmosphere and conversation within are remarkably similar and unchanging. The same cut-ups perform both in the chairs and behind them; the same badinage, political soothsaying, and sporting data are exchanged; the same amorous, if doddering, patrons furtively squeeze the hands of the same coy manicurists. One of the latter, who found it particularly difficult to laugh off the ardent advances of her chair-bound Lothario, finally told him, "Okay, I'll go to see your etchings if my husband will give his consent." "Where is this confounded husband of yours?" demanded the customer. She answered softly, "He's shaving your throat this very instant."

A lot of color went out of the barbering profession when lady practitioners dropped out of the running. The rotund and jolly TV star, Kate Smith, actually was one of the last ladies to master the tonsorial art as a little shaver (joke) in school. When she made her New York debut in a minor role in a musical in 1926, her salary didn't measure up to her appetite, so she wangled the permission of the management to do a little barbering on the side. She set up a revolving pole outside her dressing room and was soon making more in hair cutting than she was on stage. She also gave Bert Lahr the opportunity to take one look at his shorn locks in the mirror and go screaming through the wings, "Take to the hills, men! The Indians are attacking again! I've just been scalped!"

The barber pole with the spiral red stripes, incidentally, is a throwback to the time of King Henry VIII in England, when barbers were allowed also to practice minor surgery and dentistry. The red stripe presumably symbolized blood and was designed as a guide post for a majority of the citizenry who didn't know how to read. Centuries later, American barbers added a dash of blue for patriotic reasons.

When Mr. Greco moved his tonsorial parlor to the Hotel Weylin, he picked up a new assistant who was polite as all get out, but just didn't happen to be a very good barber. To one of his first customers he asked in his best Harvard accent, "Will you have anything on your face when I finish shaving you?" The customer, a crusty fellow named Knopf, answered, "I hope to save my nose, but judging by the way you're going, the odds are four to one against me."

Mr. Greco himself was shaving another customer named Colonel Pass when he paused to ask, "Well, Colonel, how do you like this new lather?" "Fine," sputtered the Colonel. "You must have lunch with *me* some day!" Undaunted, Mr. Greco demanded, "Am I not rejuvenating you? Isn't the razor taking hold?" "It's taking hold all right," admitted Colonel Pass, "but it just isn't letting go again."

The company barber, a stropping fellow, in a detachment base in Japan, tottered back to work after an epic binge in Tokyo. His first customer, a lieutenant, submitted to a shave, then inspected himself ruefully in the mirror. "If anybody tells you the Yanks aren't losing face in the Orient," he suggested, "send him round to get a look at me."

C is for the

CHILDREN'S HOUR

A dapper New Yorker—one of the ten best-dressed men in America—came to collect his six-year-old daughter at a birthday party. Taking hold of her hand to guide her across the street, he observed, "Goodness, Vicki, your hands seem mighty sticky today." "Yours would be, too," she informed him, "if you had a piece of lemon pie and a chocolate éclair inside your muff."

Film producer Eddie Knopf's son came home from college at the age of 18 with a set of marks so glittering that the whole family glowed with pride. His brother Jonathan, then five, finally felt it was time for him to get into the act, however, and declared, "I got an 'A' today in arithmetic."

His father indulgently replied, "I didn't know they taught arithmetic in kindergarten. What's one and one?" Jonathan pondered a moment, then reported, "We haven't gotten that far yet."

On the maid's day out, a prominent publisher volunteered to take the heat off his wife and tackle the Herculean task of putting their four-year-old to bed. The exhausted wife threw herself on the chaise longue and picked up the evening papers. An hour later the four-year-old stole into the room and whispered, "Daddy's asleep at last!"

Two intrepid explorers met in the heart of the Brazilian jungle. "I'm here," declared one, "to commune with nature in the raw, to contemplate the eternal verities and to widen my horizons. And you, sir?"

"I," sighed the second explorer, "came because my young daughter has begun piano lessons."

Mr. Jones' pretty, twelve-year-old daughter came screaming around the corner of the house, with the neighbor's boy in hot pursuit. Mr. Jones leaped out of his hammock and halted the two. "Why are you chasing my Gwendolyn?" he asked the, boy. "She pinched me," he complained. Mr. Jones turned to Gwendolyn. "Why did you pinch him?" he demanded. Gwendolyn answered demurely, "So he'd chase me."

A Beacon Hill youngster was showing her family album to some Boston friends from the wrong side of Commonwealth Avenue. "Isn't this one a scream?" she asked. "It's my Aunt Dorothy. She's the fattest lady who ever lived on Pinckney Street." The friend, duly impressed, said, "And who is that standing behind her?" The youngster said, "Don't be silly. That's still Aunt Dorothy."

L. Bracken, of Lakeland, Florida, sends the delectable story of the small boy who stood gazing at a horse and wagon while the milkman delivered milk. When he came out the boy observed, "Mister, that horse will never get you home." "And pray, why not?" asked the milkman. The small boy explained, "He just lost all his gasoline."

When Frank Pace, Jr., was Secretary of the Army, his wife pointed out that her husband's close association with the President and other responsible men in Government provided an excellent opportunity to give their young daughters a first-hand lesson on current events. "It is important that even the children know as much as possible these days about the tensions and problems that beset the world," urged Mrs. Pace. Frank agreed that there was great merit in his wife's proposal, and forthwith summoned his two young daughters, Paula and Priscilla, for lesson number one. The two girls were completely absorbed in his discourse. At its conclusion he asked if they had understood everything he had told them. The older daughter nodded yes. The younger—about six—admitted that one thing was bothering her very much. "Out with it," said Pace. "What is it you don't understand?" "Tell me, Daddy," she begged, "is President Truman a boy or a girl?"

A five-year-old lad in Minnesota was watching his mother change the baby. When she overlooked sprinkling the tot's backside with talcum powder and hurried him into his diaper, the five-year-old reproved her sharply, "Hey, Mom, you forgot to salt him!"

A lady who lives in Irvington-on-the-Hudson has a small son who fell out of a rowboat on a pond near the family mansion and came back to the house soaked from head to foot. She told him he must stay in his room until she could dry out his suit and iron it for him. A little later she heard a commotion in the cellar. Exasperated, she left the ironing board, and called down from the top of the basement stairs, "Are you down there wetting your pants again?" There was dead silence for a moment. Then a deep masculine voice answered meekly, "No, ma'am, I'm just reading the meter."

Oscar Levant's eight-year-old daughter, Lorna, hears the names of famous movie personages used in casual conversation at all hours of the day. Small wonder that when she saw a pair of twin boys dressed exactly alike, in a carriage in front of the Hampshire House, she exclaimed brightly, "Look, Daddy! The Warner Brothers!"

A dear little old lady entered a suburban bungalow and found a lad of four in sole possession, playing with his toy train. "You don't know me," said the old lady, "but I'm your grandmother— on your father's side." Without looking up from his train, the lad replied, "I'll tell you right now: you're on the wrong side."

A farmer in Maryland collared his nine-year-old son and demanded, "Who chopped down that there cherry tree?" The lad hung his head and admitted, "I did, Father dear. I cannot tell a lie. I chopped it with this little hatchet." The father thereupon hoisted the lad across his knees and whaled the what-for out of him. "But, Father," cried the outraged son, "George Washington cut down a cherry tree when he was a boy, too, and when he was manly enough to admit it, his father didn't wallop him. In fact, he wrote the story down for other little boys to study." "That is quite correct," said the father grimly, "but when George Washington chopped down the tree, his poor old father wasn't in it."

The teacher of a class of six-year-old girls in a progressive school found a suspicious puddle in the coat closet and demanded that the culprit step forward and identify herself. When no confession was forthcoming, the teacher registered deep disappointment and said, "Now, we're all going to close our eyes for three minutes. When we open them I confidently expect that the little girl who is guilty will be standing up at her desk." The three minutes passed, but when the class opened its eyes, no guilty little girl, alas, was standing at her desk. What the teacher did discover, however, was a second puddle next to the first in the coat closet, with a crudely lettered sign reading, "The green phantom strikes again!"

"Who says there's nothing in heredity?" demands Allen Saunders, the Toledo artist. There was a baby born in a Toledo hospital whose parents were two of the most expert and incorrigible pickpockets in the annals of Ohio crime. When the baby was two hours old, the doctors were still unable to pry open its right fist, and the mother wailed, "He's going to be deformed!" The nurse made a supreme effort, however, and bent back the infant's tiny fingers. In the palm of its hand was the obstetrician's gold watch.

Parents whose children fail to appreciate their genius may take heart from this story of Songstress Dinah Shore's baby daughter. Every time Dinah tries to sing one of her ten-thousand-dollar songs for the child, the latter begins a dreadful caterwauling, exclaiming, "Don't you sing! I want Nursie to sing for me!"

A mother of eleven unruly kids was visited by a sympathetic social worker who marveled, "How on earth are you able to care for all eleven of these children?" The mother explained, "When I only had one, he occupied every second of my time. What more can eleven do?"

Columnist Bob Considine boasts that his sons are the best-mannered lads on Ninety-sixth Street. "I've never had to lay hands on one of them," he declares, "—except in self-defense."

Arthur Krock, ace Washington news hawk, rated an invitation to a shindig at Senator Harry Byrd's Virginia manse. What's more, the Senator sent his family chariot around to give Krock a lift. Krock reports that a ferocious-looking Great Dane was

sprawled across the front seat, while the rear seat was loaded with a bevy of the Senator's small grandchildren. After some hesitation, he decided it was safer to cast his lot with the kids in back. It was a grievous error. The car had just about gotten under way when one of the kids bit him.

The Sunday-school teacher was recounting the story of the death of Joseph. When she finished, an undertaker's son raised his hand and asked, "Do you happen to know who got the funeral?"

A clever mother gave her eight-year-old son a wrist watch so that he could time himself when he practiced on the piano. A few days later the son enthused, "Gee, Mom, this watch is great. If I wind it up tight enough it does an hour in fifty-two minutes."

A little boy had been pawing over a stationer's stock of greeting cards for some time when a clerk asked, "Just what is it you're looking for, sonny? Birthday greeting? Message to a sick friend? Anniversary congratulations to your ma and dad?" The boy shook his head "no" and answered wistfully, "Got anything in the line of blank report cards?"

The eight-year-old daughter of a wealthy Park Avenue family was obsessed with fine clothes. She learned to read from the expensive fashion magazines, cut out pictures of fur coats for her scrap-book, and preferred window shopping to romping in the park. One day her mother decided the time had come to acquaint her with the facts of life and told her about the bees and flowers, et cetera, et cetera. The eight-year-old listened carefully, nodded her head, then remarked, "One thing you didn't tell me, Mama. What kind of a dress does a girl wear for a thing like that?"

One of the nicest stories I've heard in a long time concerns a writer who, through no fault of his own, lost two fine jobs in the space of a single year.

First, the magazine on which he served as managing editor folded, and then the newspaper to which he transferred was bought by a syndicate, with the casualty list embracing the entire staff.

He came home to his wife and three small sons and told them ruefully, "I'm out of a job again. The paper stopped publishing with this evening's edition." The wife comforted him as best she could. The three boys stared at him round-eyed.

Next morning the writer arose after the boys had left for school and wandered into his study.

In the wastebasket were the remains of three china piggy banks. On the dining-room table was a pile of nickels, dimes and quarters. There was a crudely lettered sign under the coins. It read, "We believe in you, Pop."

C is for
CHRISTMAS

The trouble with most Yuletide stories is that you hear them after the holidays are over, when they can no longer provide you with the maximum mileage. I suggest that you memorize a few of the following along about September or October, so you can do your Christmas swapping early.

Despite the best efforts of child psychiatrists, there are still a lot of kids of four or five—even in sophisticated New York—who believe in Santa Claus.

One of them was taken by his mother to the toy department in Macy's on a December morning last year and was duly propped up on Santa's lap. "What do you want for Christmas, my lad?" asked Santa Claus dutifully. "Better write it down," said the lad, "or you'll forget." "Trust me," urged Santa. "My memory never fails." The lad was dubious, but catalogued his demands.

The same afternoon, mother and son arrived at Gimbel's and the lad found himself on Santa's lap for a second time. The Gimbel Santa asked the usual question. "What do you want for Christmas?"

The lad slipped off his lap, kicked him lustily in the shin, and yelled, "You numskull, I *knew* you'd forget!"

In Hollywood, of course, they are faced with a different set of problems. One winsome child star instructed her private secretary, "Miss Kennedy, kindly take a letter: 'Dear Santa Claus . . .'" Another took her first ride on a department-store escalator and raised such a fuss they had to order her one for Christmas.

A star accepted a fat part in a Chicago company of a hit play, though it meant closing up his Hollywood home and moving his family to Chicago.

On October first, eve of the family's departure for the East, the star's wife told friends, "We'll have our hands full getting settled in Chicago, so I bought all my friends' Christmas presents this week." A luscious starlet regarded her with wonder and demanded, "But, my dear, how do you know who your friends will *be* by Christmastime?"

Ah, the happy Yuletide spirit! One scout reports that Mrs. Lodadoe bought Mr. Lodadoe a sixty-eight-foot yacht for a Christmas surprise last season and instructed the salesman, "Be sure to wrap it so he can't guess what it is." Mrs. Bemish called to her husband, "Last year we sent Mother a chair. What do you think we ought to do for her this year?" Mr. Bemish called back, "Electrify it." At a busy Chicago intersection a little cherub gave Santa's whiskers a yank, allowed them to snap smartly back into place. Santa retaliated by taking a pass at the cherub with his bell. He missed and landed instead on the noggin of another lad. The latter's father promptly dropped Saint Nick for a count of nine with a roundhouse right, and was in turn conked by a sturdy representative of the Chicago police force. When peace on earth

and good will to men had been restored, Santa was in jail and two
of the others were in the hospital.

The morning after Christmas, a harassed mother called in to
her husband while he was shaving, "Remember that unbreakable
toy you gave Vicki yesterday?" "I certainly do," he replied. "Don't
tell me she's succeeded in breaking it already?"

"Not at all," said the mother grimly. "She's just broken all her
other toys with it."

A French countess arrived here on the *Liberté* last year just in
time to spend the holidays on a New England farm loaned to her
by a Wall Street banker. Her friends ordered a variety of Christmas trinkets to be delivered to her by the local merchants. Word
soon went around that every time the countess answered the
bell, her feet were bound up in long strips of sheeting. One merchant, more curious than most, finally asked her why.

"Maybe I no understand your language so good," explained the
countess. "But on ze radio zey tell me veree plainly whenever
countree ladee receive visitor, she should keep ze dogs tied up."

D is for
DOCTORS

A buxom lady tripped on the stairs and broke her leg. The doctor put it in a cast and warned her that she wasn't to attempt going up or down stairs until it came off. Four months later he removed the cast and pronounced her well on the way to recovery.

"Goody, goody," gurgled the lady. "Is it all right for me to walk the stairs now?" "Yes," said the doctor, "if you will promise to be careful."

"I can't tell you what a relief it will be," confessed the lady. "It was such a nuisance crawling outside and shinnying up and down that drainpipe all the time!"

According to Sam Levenson, an irate mother marched her ten-year-old son into a doctor's office and demanded, "Is a boy of this age able to perform an appendix operation?" "Of course not," snapped the doctor. Mama turned angrily on the boy and shouted, "So who was right? Put it back!"

Mr. Malcolm's wife was dead for a full year, and still the bereaved widower showed no signs of recovering his spirits.
48

Alarmed friends persuaded him to consult an analyst. After a long talk, the analyst said, "No wonder you're melancholy! A man of your age needs some female companionship." Malcolm protested this would be unfaithful to the memory of his departed wife, but the analyst scoffed, "Nonsense! The living cannot exist on memories. Get yourself a girl. I prescribe this as your doctor." Half convinced, Malcolm announced sheepishly that he didn't even know a girl. "That's easily remedied," said the analyst, reaching for a pad and pencil. "Just take this slip to Mary McGuire at 932 East Sixty-first Street, and she'll be glad to go out with you."

Mr. Malcolm found Miss McGuire's company satisfactory in every respect. As he was bidding her an affectionate adieu, she reminded him, "Most of my boy friends leave a little gift. Shall we say twenty-five dollars?" Mr. Malcolm was rather taken aback, but rallied quickly. "Okay," he said, "here's the twenty-five, but I'd like a written receipt if you don't mind. I belong to the Blue Shield Health Plan, and they take care of all my medical expenses."

The fattest woman Throat Specialist Sulzberger ever had seen waddled into his office one afternoon and demanded an examination. The good doctor absent-mindedly said, "Okay, open your mouth, please, and say 'moo.'"

"Quick!" ordered Dr. Fitch. "My bag of pills and a stomach pump! A fellow just called up and told me he couldn't live without me." "Daddy," his daughter informed him demurely, "I believe that call was for me."

The greatest surgeon in town was performing a difficult operation before a gallery of fascinated internes. At the most crucial moment another doctor tapped the surgeon on the shoulder and asked, "May I cut in?"

Frank Brookhauser vows that the chairman of a meeting of throat specialists in Philadelphia declared on the platform, "You now have all heard the motion. All in favor say 'ah.'"

An accountant in Duluth swallowed his glass eye and rushed to a stomach specialist. The latter peered down the unfortunate fellow's throat and exclaimed, "I've looked into a lot of stomachs in my day, but I must say this is the first one that ever looked back at me."

A fashionable Park Avenue doctor recently entertained Beatrice Lillie at a soirée, and served lobster salad as the main course. "I find this so hard to digest," said Miss Lillie to her host. "Do you really like it?" The doctor assured her, "I not only like lobster salad. I'm grateful to it."

Dr. Pullman, the society dentist, tried desperately to soothe his richest but most difficult patient, a Mrs. Gruber. "Don't shake your arms like a semaphore and make those faces at me," he begged. "I haven't even started drilling yet." "I know you haven't," said Mrs. Gruber, "but you're standing on my corns."

Feeling old and discouraged? The snap of youth gone from your stride? Look over these statistics compiled by an agency pushing old-age annuity policies, and take heart: Between the ages of 75 and 83 Commodore Vanderbilt added 100 million dollars to his fortune. Kant wrote his philosophical masterpiece at 74. Tintoretto painted his biggest and most famous canvas when he was 75. Verdi was 85 when he wrote "Ave Maria." Cato decided to study Greek when he was 80. Goethe was also 80 when he finished *Faust*. And—listen to this!—Titian painted his historic "The Battle of Lepanto" when he was exactly 98!

Sun shining a bit brighter?

A hospital patient gazed fondly at his winsome, red-headed nurse and told the doctor, "Wonderful nurse you've got here. One touch of her hands cooled my fever miraculously." "We know," the doctor answered him. "We could hear her slap clear to the end of the corridor."

Bernard Gimbel, millionaire merchant and sportsman, tells about three octogenarians who were asked with whom they'd like to be buried. "John D. Rockefeller," said the first. "He not only made fortunes, but gave them away." "Franklin D. Roosevelt," said the second. "He was one of the greatest Presidents of all time." The third old man said, "My choice is Marillyn Monroe." "But Marillyn Monroe isn't dead yet," pointed out the questioner. "I know," was the answer. "Neither am I."

The Rorschach test is widely used by psychiatrists today to get an insight into the mentality and personality of new patients. The test consists of a series of cards, with different abstract designs thereon, which are shown to the patient one by one. The patient must report what each design suggests to him, and from his answers, sometimes short, sometimes wandering on for long stretches, the experienced analyst can draw a number of pertinent conclusions. The test is named after its Swiss inventor, Dr. Hermann Rorschach. There comes from the Bronx the story of one analyst who decided to use the Rorschach test on a troublesome new case. He flashed the first card on the bewildered patient and asked quietly, "Now what does this design suggest to you?" The patient peered at it a moment, then begged, "Look, Doctor, we both went to P.S. 46, didn't we? Give me a hint!"

A lady of forty discovered she was going to have a baby, and broke into loud lamentations. "I have sons of nineteen and eighteen away at college," she wailed, "and I certainly don't want another baby at this stage of the game." "You have nothing to worry about," soothed her doctor. "Forty is a good age for a mother to bear a child. I promise everything will go smoothly." "It's not the baby's birth that's upsetting me," the patient announced vehemently. "What I simply cannot face is the thought of going through that whole routine with the Parent-Teachers Association all over again!"

A friend, week-ending at a prominent psychoanalyst's home, noted a peculiar-looking butler in attendance who at least added spice to the activities by deliberately tripping up guests, fellow servants, and even his employer. As the analyst picked himself up from his third trip of the day, tenderly caressing a growing bump on his noggin, the friend burst out, "Why don't you do something about that crazy butler's tripping up everybody?" The analyst informed him coldly, "Why should I? That's *his* problem." (Later the friend predicted, "That doctor is riding for a fall. He's getting too big for his couch.")

A worried merchant sought the aid of a psychiatrist, explaining, "All day long I eat grapes." "So what?" scoffed the analyst. "Everybody eats grapes." The merchant gasped, "What? Off the *wallpaper?*"

Another patient's complaint was that he found himself slowly going mad over beautiful women. "Doc," he begged, "isn't there some way of speeding up the process?"

In California, a family of live-wire gypsies rented a store and attracted land-office business with a sign reading, "FORTUNES TOLD: $1; PSYCHOANALYSIS: 75 CENTS EXTRA."

Just before old Doc Lytton retired and turned the practice over to his son, he reminded the newly graduated young man, "One thing you got to bear in mind with patients in a small town, my boy. They find it hard sometimes to describe their symptoms accurately to you. Others hold back important details out of fear, bashfulness, or sheer orneriness. You gotta keep your eyes open and notice significant details for yourself.

"Take the case of fat Mrs. Jones, for example. Only thing wrong with her is that she stuffs herself full of candy all day. How do I know? You'll always see a dozen half empty boxes scattered all over the house. And Mr. Duncan. Liquor's at the bottom of that attack he had last night. I happened to notice an empty gin bottle in his trash basket. By observing details like that, you'll save yourself a heap of diagnosing!"

"I get it," said the son. The pair were about to enter the apartment of a luscious damsel who tossed fretfully about her bed. The new medico listened to her accentuated heartbeat, felt her fevered brow, then whipped out his thermometer. It slipped from his hands, but he recovered it quickly. Finally he told the damsel, "Nothing wrong with you that you can't cure by cutting down on your political activity. I think you're taking that part of your life a bit too seriously."

When they were back on the street, Doc Lytton asked his boy, "Where did you get the notion she was mixing too heavily in politics?"

"I just followed your tip about keeping my eyes open," said the son. "When I reached down to pick up that thermometer I'd dropped, *I saw the Governor under the bed.*"

E is for

EUROPE
And Other Continents

A bejeweled duchess waddled out of Claridge's Hotel in London where she had been cavorting—and eating—all evening at a big charity ball. As she stepped into her Rolls-Royce a beggar sidled up to her and whined, "Spare me a sixpence, m'lady, for charity. I ain't 'ad a bite for three days." The duchess recoiled. "You ungrateful fellow," she exclaimed. "Don't you realize I've been dancing for you all night?"

Lord Beaverbrook today is the all-powerful proprietor of a chain of great British newspapers. In his home town of Newcastle, New Brunswick, however, he is remembered as plain Max Aitken, inordinately ambitious son of a Presbyterian minister, and quite definitely outside the social swim. He engineered his first big "deal" when he was ten. A soap company offered prizes to lads who amassed the biggest collection of wrappers. Young Max took all of his savings out of the bank, bought soap by the case from the factory, and sold it by the cake at wholesale prices with the proviso that purchasers turn the wrappers over to him. Needless to say, he won first prize—a bicycle—by the proverbial mile.

There still lives in Newcastle an aged socialite who once kept Beaverbrook from membership in the local club. This summer he called Beaverbrook on the evening of his arrival and asked if he might have the pleasure of giving a dinner in his honor. "That's not possible, thank you," answered Beaverbrook, and could not resist adding, "You see, I'm expected to rejoin the King and Queen."

Jack Benny tells a good story on himself that came out of his first personal appearance in London's famous Palladium Theatre. The whole town turned out for the event, including London's No. 1 drama critic and his wife.

The critic liked Benny fine, but his wife watched him with a puzzled frown for a full twenty minutes and then whispered to her husband, "Tell me, dear, what does Mr. Benny do?"

J. B. Priestley tells about a dour-visaged, portly farmer from the Midland country in England who lumbered into the headquarters of the Tory Party in London and inquired, "How much does it cost to join?" "A half guinea," an official replied, "but surely you haven't waited until this stage of your life to become a member of the conservatives?" "That I haven't," the farmer exclaimed, "but it was only when the damn Labour Government came into power I was able to afford it!"

Socialized medicine is one of the accomplishments on which the British Labour Party prides itself most. Members of the American Medical Association, horrified that something of the same nature may be on its way over here, will like the story of what happened to one young married lady in London who believed that she was in the family way and went to the Public Health Station to make sure. The doctor there gave her a cursory examination, assured her that her suspicions were well founded, and then, to her astonishment, simply took a rubber stamp, printed something with it on her abdomen, and said "That's all."

She reported the strange goings-on to her husband that evening, and he, of course, asked, "What does it say?" "I can't read it," she admitted. He, too, found upon inspection that the print was too small for him, but a magnifying glass made everything clear. The inscription was, "When you can read this *without* a magnifying glass, rush your wife to the hospital."

An English gourmet ordered several baskets of succulent French snails, but found the customs tariff on "horned animals" exorbitant. So he crossed out "horned animals," classified them as "prefabricated houses" and brought them in duty free!

Colonel Effingham was walking to his club late one night in London when an ebony-hued hussy stepped out of the shadows, linked her arm in his, and said, "How would you like to take me home?" The startled colonel stared at her in horror and exclaimed, "Good heavens, girl, all the way to *Africa?*"

An American tourist in England asked the gardener at Kensington Gardens, "How do you ever get lawns as perfect as that?" The reply was, "Well, madam, the first thing you have to do is begin about 600 years ago."

When a Londoner wants an old-fashioned, pre-war meal these days, he flies over to Ireland to get it—if he can afford the trip, of course. One brought home the story of a stubborn old Dubliner who staggered into a dentist's office with a whopper of a toothache, but couldn't quite muster sufficient courage to have the infected molar extracted. The dentist poured him a stiff shot of whiskey to bolster his morale, then asked, "Ready now?" "Not quite yet," said the afflicted one with a smack of his lips. Two more slugs of whiskey found him still reluctant so the dentist let him polish off the bottle. "Now step into the chair," he begged. The Irishman, however, came out swinging to the middle of the room. "I'd like to see the confounded rascal," he bellowed, "who'd dare touch me teeth now."

Up in Scotland, a golfer stepped to the first tee, and sliced his ball so badly that it crashed through a window of the clubhouse way off to the right. He rushed to retrieve it, and found a half dozen fellow members in a dither of excitement. "Darnedest ricochet in the history of St. Albans," marveled one. "After that ball broke the window, it bounced off Mrs. McIntosh's head, knocked over MacTavish's whiskey and soda, bounced through another window, and broke the rector's windshield." "Never mind all the chatter," said the golfer severely. "Where's my ball now?"

One of the big manufacturers of plaids and tartans in Edinburgh received word that its traveling salesman had expired suddenly in a Liverpool hotel. The manager in Edinburgh wired—collect: "Return samples by freight and search his pants for orders."

Mrs. McDermott looked out of the window as the family was going on to dinner, and wailed, "Och, Sandy, here comes company. I bet they haven't eaten yet." Sandy, equal to the emergency, ordered, "Quick! Everybody out on the porch—with a toothpick."

The immigration authorities at Ellis Island were examining the credentials of a middle-aged Scotch couple that sought admission to our shores. The passport pictures caused trouble. "Mr. Mac-Gregor," said the official, "this photograph of you is a perfect likeness, but I must say this other picture looks nothing like Mrs. MacGregor to me. Have you other substantiating evidence that this lady with you is indeed your wife?"

Mr. MacGregor sighed deeply and whispered to the official, "Laddie, if ya can prove she isn't, I'll gie ya twenty pounds."

King Christian of Denmark has been making a good-will tour through every hamlet in his little kingdom. In one village fully five hundred children waved flags and pelted him with flowers. "Where on earth do all these children come from?" laughed the King. "Your Majesty," the local mayor assured him gravely, "we have been making preparations for this day for ten years!"

En route by automobile to the Riviera in Southern France, movie tycoon Darryl Zanuck stayed overnight at a small inn south of Vichy. "You must fill out registration papers for the local gendarmes," the proprietor reminded him. "It is the law, you know." "I'm tired of these darn forms and regulations," said Zanuck. "Fill it out for me. My full name is on all the baggage." He went upstairs to refresh himself, and upon returning was presented with his filled-out registration form. The first line read, "Monsieur Warranted Genuine Leather."

A Western congressman who has been screaming continuously for expanded American financial accommodations to the Franco dictatorship in Spain went over to Madrid to inspect conditions for himself—and anybody who says he knew in advance he was going to find everything just hunky-dory is being deliberately unkind. When he returned to Washington an opponent challenged, "Well, how much do the Spaniards themselves respect their ruler?" "They're crazy about him," enthused the congressman. "I rode all over with him for three days in an open car and not a single shot was fired at either of us."

Seeking to steer clear of the Soviet orbit, Eliezer Kaplan, the finance minister of the very young state of Israel, journeyed to these shores recently to float a five-hundred-million-dollar bond issue.

The directors of a conservative Wall Street banking house listened courteously to his story, and then the chairman asked him, "Would it be possible, Mr. Kaplan, to let us see Israel's last three annual balance sheets?"

Kaplan answered, "The last two, Mr. Chairman, I can produce without difficulty. The one before that, I am afraid, disappeared when the Temple was destroyed in 586 B.C.!"

Two ancients in Israel were bemoaning the hardships of living in the new republic. "What we should do," proposed Semmish, "is declare war on the United States. They beat us, and like they do with all defeated enemies, immediately give us money, new roads, lots of food, houses and factories." "It's no good," sighed Lazarus. "With our luck, we'd win!"

Gregory Ratoff spotted this sign in an army barracks in Israel: "Privates will kindly refrain from giving advice to officers."

In Tel-Aviv, a citizen made a fortune selling prefabricated houses, but discovered he had to pay most of it in taxes. He signed his check with a deep sigh and remarked, "Over two thousand years we wait for a Jewish home state—and it has to happen to me!"

A raconteur in Haifa began a funny story at a dinner party with the standard introduction, "It seems there were two Jewish gentlemen . . ." A sensitive guest objected. "Why," he demanded, "do so many stories begin 'Once there were two Irishmen,' or 'Once there were two Jews'?" "Okay," soothed the raconteur, "I certainly intended no offense. Let's say there were two Chinese, named Ling Pu and Fo Wang. So, Pu and Wang were hustling over to the synagogue for a bar-mitzvah ceremony . . ."

A tourist in Algiers told his guide, "I'm tired of seeing all the places you show every American. I want to see the real Africa!" The guide said, "I will take you to the wildest, most exotic café this side of the Sahara. You will never forget it!" The two men walked to a dark and forbidding house on the edge of the town and, after a certain amount of hokus-pokus at the gate, were admitted.

Several nondescript characters were draped about the premises in various abandoned attitudes, but what immediately caught the tourist's eye was an English colonel, impeccably attired, swagger stick and all, who, believe it or not, was exactly *six inches tall!* As he stared in disbelief, the bartender threw a red silk cord over the edge of the bar, the colonel pulled himself up hand over hand, and perched on the top with a whiskey and soda in his hand.

The guide was delighted. "What luck," he told the tourist.

"You're going to meet Colonel Pringle, one of the most fascinating sights in all Africa!" Then he turned to the six-inch figure and boomed, "Be a good fellow, Colonel Pringle, and tell my tourist friend here about the night you told that witch doctor to go chase himself in the lake!"

The main course at Chief Zombongo's birthday dinner was a succulent missionary who had been caught wandering in the African bush three weeks previous and specially fattened for the occasion. Scarcely had the distinguished guests arisen from the festive board, however, when Chief Zombongo was seized with a violent stomach-ache, and disappeared hastily into his private hut. He was back a half hour later, seemingly none the worse for wear, explaining to his guests, "It's like I always told you. You can't keep a good man down."

Manners are on the upgrade among the cannibals in darkest Africa. One chief was heard reproving his son, "How often have I told you not to talk with someone in your mouth?" Another chief's wife became interested in a number of worthy charities. Her husband finally refused to bring home any more guests for dinner. He explained, "I'm tired of having my wife put the bite on them."

When Timothy McElligott was cast away on a desert island with two beautiful young ladies, he thought he was the luckiest man in the world. The island provided ample food and shelter, the climate was temperate—and there didn't seem to be another human within a thousand-mile radius. Soon, however, McElligott realized there was a fly in the ointment. The beautiful young ladies made constant demands: he had to set up a strict schedule: Mondays, Wednesdays and Fridays to make one happy; Tuesdays, Thursdays and Saturdays for the other. Sundays he reserved for general overhauling and resting his weary bones.

While fishing one day, McElligott was overjoyed to observe another shipwrecked sailor drifting ashore on a raft. "What luck— and just in time," he told himself. To the sailor he hallooed, "Welcome, mister. You'll love it here." The sailor answered, "For goodness sake, I should hope so. I'm in a perfect snit about the way that nasty sun has burned me. I hope you have some vanishing cream on this beastly island."

"Heaven help me," prayed McElligott, "here go my Sundays!"

A visitor from Australia walked into the Rolls-Royce showroom and paid cash on the line for the most expensive limousine model. "Ship it to my sheep ranch outside of Sydney," he instructed the sales manager. A year later he was back to order another car. "Best model I ever saw," he exclaimed, "and you can quote me on that. I particularly approve of the glass partition between the

front and rear seats. Most ingenious feature of the whole car."
"Why do you say that?" inquired the Rolls-Royce representative.
"It's like this," explained the Australian. "I roll that window up,
and I'd like to see the damn sheep that can lick the back of my
neck while I'm driving it to market!"

When Juan and Evita Perón were building a luxurious retreat
for themselves some miles outside of Buenos Aires they established a rigid guard around the project to prevent the stealth of
valuable materials. Every day at noon, the story goes, the same
workman began to appear at the exit gate with a wheelbarrow
loaded with straw. The guard, convinced that there was dirty
work afoot, searched the straw more carefully daily—even had it
analyzed to see if it possessed special chemical values—but could
find nothing to substantiate his suspicion, and had to let the
workman pass.

A year later, the guard met the workman, evidently enjoying
great prosperity. "Now that all is said and done," pleaded the
guard, "just what were you stealing every day on that Perón project?" The workman whispered, "Wheelbarrows."

Before China was engulfed by the Red tide, a family named
Lum—grandfather, father and twelve-year-old son—lived in pov-
erty in a tiny compound. The grandfather was crippled by arthritis and unable to continue his share of work in the rice paddy, so
the father decided to liquidate him. He trussed him up in a big
market basket and made for the shore of the Yangtze River. En
route he met his son who cried, "What are you doing to my poor
grandfather?" "Quiet," whispered the father. "By lowering him
into the stream we will end his suffering and at the same time
lighten our load." "I see," nodded the son, "but be sure to bring
back the basket. I'll need it for you one day."

F is for FARMERS

A New Hampshire farmer was so contented on his own little rocky plot of ground that he had ventured to the nearest city, Portsmouth, only five times in his life. On his last visit he suffered a painful experience. A fire siren sounded, and he hastily steered his horse and buggy over to the curbstone. When the engine had clanged by he proceeded on his way, only to be smacked squarely in the rear by the hook-and-ladder truck. When the doctors restored the poor man to consciousness they asked, "Why didn't you get out of the way? You must have heard the siren." "I heard it all right," he answered grimly, "but it wasn't the durn engine that hit me at all. It was that truckload of crazy house-painters careening along behind it!"

Farmer Jepson came storming out of the house brandishing his shotgun and shouting, "Dad bust it, Ezry Jones, I told you to quit courtin' my daughter. Now you git into that mangy old truck of yours, and git off my property once and for all." Ezry discreetly released Miss Jepson from his arms, and climbed into his truck—but as he drove off he had the last word. "You old skinflint," he jeered, "I'd run right over you if I wasn't scairt of puncturin' all my tires."

Nick Agropopolus, who did a mite of farming down Maryland way, received a notice from the town council that the license to maintain a cow on his premises had expired. Agropopolus took pen in hand and replied, "My cow she beat you to it. She expire two weeks ago. Much oblige: Your truly . . ."

In Washington, a government survey was ordered to study the migratory habits of birds. Thousands of all species were released with metal strips attached reading, "Notify Fish and Wild Life Division. Wash. Biol. Surv." Hugh Newton writes, "The abbreviation was changed abruptly following receipt of this penciled note from a vexed Alberta agriculturist: 'Gents: I shot one of your crows last week and followed instructions attached to it. I washed it, biled it, and surved it. It was awful. You should stop trying to fool the public with things like this.'"

Governor Luther Youngdahl, of Minnesota, says that the stingiest man in his bailiwick is the old Swedish-American who moseyed into a butcher shop and demanded ten cents worth of beefsteak. "But Mr. Olefson," protested the butcher, "you've got nine children. What are you going to do with the tiny scrap of meat I can give you for a dime?" "This ain't for eating purposes," explained Mr. Olefson. "I just like to have the smell in the house when company comes."

Old Pop Diggins had talked about a trip out West for twenty years, and now his dream was about to be realized. "One week from today," he exulted to his cronies at Green's General Store, "I'll be plumb in the middle of that there Yellowstone Park!" One of them cackled, "Don't you forget Old Faithful." "I won't," promised Pop Diggins. "I'm taking her with me."

An agricultural journal reports that a farmer in Wisconsin, who always complained that his wife didn't shoulder her share of the burden, agreed to run the household one day while his wife went to Madison for a medical examination. A methodical chap, he kept a minute record of his activities. It read as follows:

> Opened door for children: 106 times.
> Shouted, "Stop, Johnnie": 94
> Tied their shoes: 16
> Stopped quarrels: 19
> Provided glasses of water and cokes: 26
> Answered phone: 11
> Answered questions: 202
> Ran after children: about 4½ miles
> Lost temper: 45 times.

The next day the farmer himself journeyed to Madison—and bought his wife the washing machine she had long coveted.

Kenneth Roberts is a novelist of parts, the author of such best sellers as *Northwest Passage* and *Lydia Bailey*. When a man of his stature solemnly assures us that he believes in dowsing rods and the sensitive souls who manipulate same, it behooves us at least to examine his claims with an open mind.

A dowser is a man who can hold between his fingers any flexible Y-shaped tree branch and, by extending it straight in front of him, theoretically detect the presence of water. Through no effort of his own, the rod is supposed to turn downward with irresistible force the moment he passes above a spot where the subterranean sheets of water exist.

In his book, *Henry Gross and His Dowsing Rod*, Mr. Roberts details (with a host of corroborating witnesses) exploits of a Maine neighbor that certainly seem to tag him the real McCoy. However, scientific skeptics still hold to their story that it can't be done.

When Mr. Roberts first encountered Henry Gross, the nine springs on the writer's farm were wholly inadequate. Gross simply marched across the property with his forked stick and told Roberts exactly where to dig new wells. Now he has not only all the drinking water he needs, but a sizable pond besides.

By not sparing his rod, Mr. Gross even was able to tell the writer how far down in the earth the water would be found and how fast it flowed.

To cap the climax, and prove that Mr. Gross is the super-duper dowser of them all, he plunked himself down in a chair in Roberts' Kennebunkport, Me., library and waved his rod over a map of Bermuda. He located three sources of water on a tract of land where geologists and test drillers had sworn that not a drop of uncontaminated fresh water existed. And were their faces red when Mr. Gross's prediction held water!

Mr. Gross's rod, admits Kenneth Roberts, has its limitations as far as hard liquor is concerned. When touched to rye before being put to use, it works only on rye thereafter, ignoring any quantity of Scotch, blended whiskey, or Jack Daniel's Number Seven Sour Mash. This strikes me as a very minor defect. Any man who can't tell Number Seven without a dowsing rod doesn't deserve good liquor.

The dowsing rod behaved in exemplary fashion the day it was exhibited in a big Boston department store. Mr. Gross extended it before him and sallied forth. The rod led him unerringly to the ladies' washroom.

Farmer Thomas' barn had just gone up in smoke, and his insurance agent was trying to explain that he couldn't collect cash for it. "Read the policy," he insisted. "All our company engages to do is build you another barn exactly like the one that's been destroyed."

Farmer Thomas, apoplectic with rage, thundered, "If that's the way you varmints do business, cancel the policy on my wife before it's too late."

A fellow down in Pumpkin Creek bet a city slicker ten dollars he could ride the flywheel in a new sawmill. His widow, paying off the bet after the funeral, observed, "Cal was a right good husband, but he sure didn't know beans about flywheels."

Farmer Klopfer sidled into the general store at Flemington with a look of acute melancholy on his face. "I kin tell by looking at you," said the knowing proprietor of the store, "that that danged old mule of yours has been acting up again." "You hit the nail right on the head," admitted Klopfer, reaching for a plug of chewing tobacco. "You'll never listen to me," said the proprietor. "Didn't I tell you that the next time that critter balked you should just build a fire under him and *make* him move?" "That's just what I done," complained Farmer Klopfer, "but that ornery beast moved just fur enough to pull the wagon over the fire and burn it up."

Art Noble dropped into our office the other day with a clipping from an Arkansas paper that read, "A roaring twister last Tuesday carried off John Squire's house and furniture. All four of his children are missing. Neighbors promptly donated a new bed to give John and his wife for a fresh start." . . . Art also told us that alert folks out his way have finally figured out why a farmer looks for a needle in a haystack. Seems that's where the farmer's daughter frequently does her fancy work.

My Uncle Herbert loves to rough it in the woods every summer, communing with nature in an outfit that sets him back about three hundred dollars at Abercrombie and Fitch. Last year we were gradually freezing to death in an overnight cabin in Maine when I suggested that Uncle Herbert blaze a trail to the kitchen and light the stove. A couple of moments later he was back with his impeccable costume strangely tattered and torn. "I thought you were going to light the stove?" I grumbled. "I did," maintained Uncle Herbert, "but it went out." "Well," I said impatiently, "light it again." "I can't," said Uncle Herbert. "It went out through the roof."

"My garden was such a success this year," boasted a gentleman farmer, "that my neighbor's chickens took first prize at the poultry show."

Reminded that Henry Ford had left an estate of over a hundred million dollars, an Iowa deacon shook his head slowly and observed, "Strikes me he must have had an awful savin' woman."

Barbara Anne, a freshman at Wellesley, came home to her tiny home town for Christmas, and hastened to tell her father who was waiting at the station to bundle her into the family station wagon, "Paw, there's something you might as well know right off. I ain't a good girl any more." Paw clapped one hand to his forehead and cried out, "Twenty years your maw and I have made sacrifices so's you could go to a smart Eastern college, and what happens? You come home after three full months there—and you're still saying 'ain't'!"

Hoagy Carmichael is responsible for the story of the crack shot of an Indiana community who was never over-modest in retailing legends of his prowess. On one hunting trip, the marksman took careful aim and fired, but the bird sailed on undisturbed into the blue. The marksman watched it in dazed silence for a moment,

then dashed his gun to the ground, and cried out, "Fly on, you blankety-blank fool bird! Fly on with your gol-durned heart shot out!"

In the feuding country of the Blue Ridge Mountains, the Abernathys and the Spillanes shot at each other on sight for three generations. Townsfolk thought they might end the feud by appointing the heads of the two families joint mayors. The ancient enemies shook hands, then rushed forth to try to outdo each other in sartorial splendor at the inauguration ceremony. Old Tod Abernathy decided to wear the cutaway and striped trousers in which deceased males of his clan were laid out before burial. Thus adorned, he entered the kitchen to collect his womenfolk. His wife took one horrified look at him and cried, "Dawgone! Them Spillanes has got my Tod at last!"

An Ozark native, aged eighty or thereabouts, ambled into a doctor's office in Crane, Missouri, and announced, "Doc, I seem to have picked up a first-class case of insomnia somewhere. I keep wakin' up every few days."

Bob Uchitelle solemnly swears that this is an authentic excerpt from an Arkansas hillbilly's diary:

> March 15: Rainin', can't go huntin'!
> March 16: Still rainin', can't go huntin'!
> March 17: Still rainin'. Shot Gramma.

A native of the Ozarks was asked by a revenue agent, "Seen your grandpappy lately?" The native pointed with his corncob pipe to an indistinct object at the far end of his tomato patch and said, "See that figger over thar? It's either a tree stump or grandpappy. Keep your eyes on it. If it moves, it's a tree stump."

In George Heister's home town, Colonel Lemuel Witheringham, noble scion of an aristocratic but impoverished family, was known as its most silver-tongued and long-winded orator. When he died of old age, his obit in the *Gazette* read, "The late Colonel plunged into the unfathomable, soared into the infinite, and communed with the inscrutable—but he never paid cash."

A fine distinction between acquaintanceship and friendship has been established by such Southern tobacco auctioneers as haven't been exported to New York for radio appearances. Several were convening in a backwoods bar, when a newcomer approached. One of the group patted him on the back and said, "Russ, you know Joe Arbuckle, don't you?" Russ grudgingly extended a hand, and allowed, "We've howdied but we ain't shook."

As a result of a tip from a source considered reliable, the game warden of Shuckamockie County reluctantly donned his snow shoes and mushed halfway up a mountain to corner old Hermit Hawkins, a "character" in those hills for years. He dragged his weary bones back into his home some seven hours later. "Well," said his wife, "did you find that old Hawkins really was poaching?" "Yep," he reported with a sigh. "Deer or elk?" she asked. "Eggs," said the game warden.

A worried girl came down from the mountains to tell her doctor, "We gotta do somethin' 'bout grandmaw's smokin'. She inhales." "Nothing so terrible about that, Elviry," soothed the doctor. "Plenty of women inhale nowadays." "You don't understan'," persisted Elviry. "Grandmaw don't exhale!"

Stories about a succession of child marriages in the feudin'
country down South reminded Viola Swisher of the day a Blue
Ridge mountaineer fell ill. The doctor reassured the patient's worried husband, "That little wife of yours'll be perfectly all right in
a couple of days, son. She's just teething."

That traveling salesman you've always heard about ran out of
gas one evening on a lonely road and asked at the only farmhouse
in sight (where else?), "Can you put me up for the night?" The
farmer said, "I reckon I can—if you don't mind sharing a room
with my young son." "Good heavens," gasped the salesman, "I'm
in the wrong joke!"

G is for GAMING

A young bride's honeymoon in New York turned out disastrously because her husband, an inveterate bridge fiend, insisted upon spending every minute of his time watching the play at a Master Championship Tournament.

She picked expert Oswald Jacoby to be her confidant, complaining, "I stood it till the sixty-second hand. Then I lost my temper completely and walked out on him."

"The sixty-second hand?" mused Jacoby. "That was unforgivable, my dear. The sixty-second hand was by far the most interesting hand in the tournament."

In a Western gambling dive, a tenderfoot from New England lost his stake in suspiciously quick order. On the street he was voicing his suspicions about the dive, when a tough-looking gent, sporting extensive firearms, sidled up to him.

"Are you accusin' my associates inside of runnin' a crooked joint?" he demanded.

The tenderfoot paled and explained hastily:

"Nothing of the sort. I only said that I was watching the dealer in that twenty-one game—and the card on the top of the deck struck me as mighty dusty."

A lady who cannot resist the lure of roulette wheels and slot machines stopped off at Reno on her way home from the coast, and bumped into Walter Clark, author of *The Ox-Bow Incident.* "Fancy meeting you here," exclaimed Clark. "What hotel are you staying at?" "Hotel?" echoed the lady, as she bought a new stack of chips. "My dear boy, I've only been here four days!"

The going was even rougher than usual at the Guggenheims' weekly bridge joust with the Loebs. "Will you tell me," demanded the exasperated Mrs. G. of her spouse, "how you could make an original bid of three no-trumps when I was sitting there with all four aces and a king in my hand?" "If you must know," admitted the harassed Mr. Guggenheim, "I bid on three queens, two jacks and four highballs."

Latest "kibitzer" story tells of one of the most persistent of the breed, who hovered behind a card player for three solid hours giving advice. What's more, the player won consistently. Suddenly he found himself in a quandary. Turning to the kibitzer, he whispered, "Well, smart guy, what do I play now, the ten or the queen?" The kibitzer answered, "First you've got to tell me this: What game are you playing?"

Three ladies at a Saratoga hotel, desperately seeking a fourth for bridge, finally appealed to a little old lady in an alpaca dress who was crocheting and minding her own business in a sheltered corner of the porch. Flustered but obviously pleased by the invitation, she said, "I'll play, but I warn you, I'm not up on all those new conventions." "Don't worry," they assured her. "None of us are members of the Regency Club either." On the very first hand, three consecutive passes left the bidding strictly up to the little old lady. She studied her hand carefully, cocked her head to one side, and bid, "Two clovers."

Monte Carlo was the scene of a strange occurrence one night many years ago. An elderly gentleman took a seat in the casino and ventured fifty francs on Number 17. The number came up. The old man pointed at Number 17 again and made no move to rake in any of his winnings.

Again the little silver ball came to rest at Number 17! The croupier looked questioningly at the old man, who sat with his head down on one arm and his finger pointed at Number 17 on the board. Five more consecutive times the wheel hit Number 17. The old man's pile of chips was enormous. The crowd stood silent with admiration for his nerve. The croupier had a hurried consultation with the directors, and announced that the bank was broken and the roulette game was at an end.

But the winner of the fortune never stirred. He was dead. Furthermore, a doctor testified in court he had been dead ever since the second spin. A dead man broke the bank at Monte Carlo!

Elinor Maxwell heard a young Lothario confide to the custodian of the Whaling Bar, "If I only had enough money to marry her—I'd bet every cent of it on my favorite horse!"

Mr. John McNulty, who specializes in discovering—and writing about—slightly zany characters in Third Avenue saloons and joints adjacent, is himself a somewhat erratic bettor when the horses are running. One day he was observed leaving the press box at Churchill Downs just after a long shot had come in to pay $76 for every $2 ticket. By way of being pleasant, Joe Palmer said, "I hope you had that one." Mr. McNulty answered indignantly, "At 38 to 1? Do you think I'm crazy?"

H is for
HOLLYWOOD

Do you remember the old songs and lithographs that conveyed heartbreaking stories of little girls sneaking into the family entrance of a corner saloon trying to entice papa into laying off the lager beer and free lunch and coming home to his starving family? The present-day, Hollywood version of that sad situation has for its improbable setting a special table at the luxurious Hillcrest Golf Club, with a cast of characters consisting of eleven world-famous comedians. They love one another's company and jokes so much, their children can't even persuade them to come home to cash their salary checks.

The eleven members of this ultra-exclusive fraternity are Groucho, Harpo and Chico Marx, Danny Kaye, George Jessel, Lou Holtz, George Burns, Jack Benny, and the three zany Ritz Brothers. It's unlikely that the club will grow, since the rules state explicitly that any new candidate must get fifteen affirmative votes, which is rather difficult when only eleven men are eligible to cast ballots. Golf is the least of the members' worries. Groucho's son Arthur avers that eight years after the club had been established, Holtz and Jessel found themselves on the clubhouse veranda for the first time. Jessel spotted the eighteenth green and exclaimed, "When did they put in a golf course here?" Last year the most disliked member of the Hillcrest Club dropped dead on the first tee while practicing swings with a driver. When word of this percolated back to the comedians' table, George Burns turned to Danny Kaye triumphantly and said, "I *told* you this was a tough course."

One lady member of the Hillcrest Club sits for hours at the nearest table to the group's sacred meeting spot with a hearing aid pressed to her ear. "It's the only place," she explains, "you can hear all the latest jokes without one darn commercial."

Groucho Marx, explains his brother Harpo, is infatuated with words. "Groucho," he says, "doesn't regard words the way the rest of us do. He looks at them upside down, backwards, from the middle out to the end, and from the end back to the middle. Next he drops them in a mental Mixmaster, and studies them some more. Groucho doesn't look for double meanings. He looks for quadruple meanings. And usually finds them."

One day an officious lady at the Brown Derby in Hollywood pushed a waiter aside, leveled a finger at Groucho, and demanded, "Are you Harpo Marx?" Groucho raised an eyebrow and replied, "No. Are you?"

An elderly book clerk in Hollywood is still suffering from the shock sustained when Groucho entered her shop and inquired blandly, "Have you something obscene for a seven-year-old girl?"

Groucho is said to net over $4000 a week these days with his radio and television chores, but there was a time when all four Marx brothers together had a difficult job keeping the wolf away from the door. When traveling from one town to another their mother, Minnie Marx, dressed them up in short pants and Buster Brown collars so they could ride for half fare. Once, when a harassed conductor informed Mrs. Marx that her "little boys" were smoking cigars, chasing girls, and playing poker in the coach ahead, she beamed at him and confided, "They grow so fast."

Al Shean, famous as the partner of Mr. Gallagher, was also the man responsible for making Harpo Marx a silent comedian. Shean scripted the first vaudeville act for the then-unknown Marx Brothers, and inadvertently forgot to write in a part for Harpo.

When Harpo indignantly called the omission to his attention, Shean hastily explained, "I did it on purpose. I want you to play in pantomime. I've got a feeling you'll be terrific." Mr. Shean didn't know how right he was! Incidentally, one of the first towns to see the new Marx Brothers turn was Waukegan. In the orchestra pit, a kid named Kubelsky played the fiddle, and doubled up with laughter every time Groucho opened his mouth. Today, some thirty years later, Kubelsky is still laughing at Groucho. Now, however, he is known as Jack Benny.

Groucho owes it to his legion of admirers to revive some day the classic scene in which he played Napoleon bidding farewell to a slightly bleary-eyed Josephine. "Jo," he would declare, seizing her in his arms, "your eyes shine like the seat of my blue serge pants, and I know you are as true as a three-dollar cornet. But hark, they are playing the Mayonnaise! The army must be dressing." Josephine came out of her trance to aver, "Nappy, I am true to the French army." "Thank heaven," Groucho shouted, "France has no navy."

A dashing young movie hero, delight of millions of bobby soxers, was told by his studio head, "It's time you played a different kind of role. We're casting you as a miner in your next picture." The hero announced firmly, "Nothing doing. I hate minors. The last one I met cost me fifty thousand dollars."

A near-sighted director was searching for locations for an impending farm epic when a gust of wind blew off his beret. He gave chase, but every time he apparently had it cornered, it was whisked from under his hand again. Finally a woman looked up from her gardening and called, "What are you trying to do over there, mister?" "I'm trying to recover my beret," he puffed. "Your beret is over there by the stone wall," said the woman. "That's our black hen you've been chasing."

Another near-sighted gentleman was heard moaning at a race-track bar, "I've got to get these glasses fixed fast. I've just walked into seven fellows I owe money to!"

S. Z. "Cuddles" Sakall, the rotund comedian, asked a pint-sized dancer how much she weighed. "A hundred and one," she told him. Sakall sighed and pointed out, "I ate more than that for lunch."

Cuts are so rampant in one Hollywood studio, chronicles Mike Connolly, they're signing all new contracts with styptic pencils. Mike also reports that Football Star Bob Waterfield, whose wife happens to be Jane Russell, told an interviewer, "Certainly I do the cooking. Do you think I want Jane to melt her career away over a hot stove?"

The late W. C. Fields, not noted for sobriety, was once asked if he ever had suffered delirium tremens in Hollywood. "That's impossible to answer," rasped the comedian. "It's impossible to tell where D.T.'s end and Hollywood begins." (It was Alexander Woollcott who described the whole Los Angeles area as "Seven suburbs in search of a city.")

A member of the census bureau, assigned to Hollywood, reports that the door of one sumptuous villa he visited was opened by a man in cerise pajamas. "How many people live in this house?" asked the census taker. "And what are their ages and occupations?" "How would I know?" answered the man in pajamas. "I've never been here before in my life."

Will Rogers, always down to earth and allergic to phony glamour, nevertheless had one "dream girl" whose doings he followed like any other star-struck citizen. Her name was Greta

Garbo. Will went six blocks out of his way every night on his way home from the studio just to get an occasional glimpse of Miss Garbo, and once in a while he'd get an extra dividend in the form of a wave of recognition from her. Those were red-letter days for Rogers! While Will was in New York one winter, however, Miss Garbo sold her hacienda and moved up into the more remote hills surrounding Hollywood. Thus it was that the next time Will sauntered by the old villa for a glimpse of Miss Garbo, the face on the porch belonged to his old, fat, and unglamorous friend, Irvin S. Cobb. Shocked and dismayed, Rogers made straight for a Western Union office and sent Cobb this wire: "Dearest Greta: Land sakes, gal, how you've changed."

Just last summer Miss Garbo came close to buying for herself a quaint and rambling old farmhouse on Long Ridge Road, Connecticut. At least she asked the aged owner to name a selling price. "But I don't want to sell it to you," said the owner bluntly. "I'm sure you do not understand," the actress protested. "I'm Greta Garbo." "Exactly," said the owner. "And that's why I don't want to sell my charming old house to you. You have the means to spoil it!"

A prominent and pulchritudinous starlet in Hollywood was discovered gazing blankly into space by Sid Skolsky. "Why the depression?" asked Sid. The starlet sighed deeply, then explained, "My analyst just told me I'm really in love with my father. What'll I do, Sid? He's a married man!"

A newly crowned Hollywood queen, very blonde, very sexy, told a reporter that her real love was a sixty-year-old banker in Wall Street. "Every time he phones me to the coast," she purred, "I get chinchillas up and down my spine."

Publicist Leo Guild solemnly swears that a new Warner Brothers contract player, intent upon making a big impression on her first visit to Hollywood, signed the Beverly Wilshire Hotel register, "Mary Blossom and made."

Two agents were seated at a table in Mike Romanoff's new Hollywood restaurant watching Clark Gable, Van Johnson, Dore Schary, Mervyn LeRoy and Spencer Tracy dine lengthily and well. "Look at them," sighed one of the agents. "How'd you like to have ten per cent of their salaries?" The other said, "The way things are in the film business today, I'd be satisfied with ten per cent of their dinner checks."

A fellow-producer persuaded Sam Goldwyn to attend a preview of a blood-and-thunder picture, and at its conclusion enthused, "Isn't that a real, old-fashioned swashbuckler for you?" Goldwyn wisely pointed out, "The trouble is, it buckles where it should swash!" And Moss Hart tells about the day Mr. Goldwyn asked how he was progressing with his script on the life of Hans Christian Andersen. "If you don't like the job I've done," proclaimed Moss earnestly, "I will emulate Van Gogh, cut off my ear, and present it to you." "My boy," said Goldwyn, "in my desk I've got a whole drawer full of ears. All I ask from you is a good box-office script."

One big Hollywood producer came home to find his wife sobbing uncontrollably. "That famous author of yours!" she wailed. "He came marching in this afternoon, seized me in his arms, and

despite my protests, made violent love to me for three hours."
"Hm-m-m," mused the producer, "I wonder what the so-and-so
wants?"

Things had gotten so tough for one independent producer in
Hollywood that he was filming an entire feature in four days flat.
In a final desperate gamble to recoup his fortune, he signed an
authentic star at five thousand dollars a day, and set frantically to
work. Toward the end of the second day, the cameraman reported, "Gotta stop a few moments, boss. Our star had to go to the
washroom." "Stop nothing," boomed the producer. "We'll shoot
around him!"

A Hollywood agent, usually very chipper, sat despondently at
the soda counter of Schwab's Pharmacy. "Whassamatter?" asked
a friend anxiously. "It's that new client I'm representing," groaned
the agent. "Sings like Lanza, fights like Flynn, and acts like Vic-
tor Mature." "So why do you worry," laughed the friend. "You'll
make a million out of this guy." "Guy nothing, you dope," cried
the agent. "It's a *girl!*"

I is for
INTOXICANTS

Colonel R. Juniper Bragg, asked why he always closed his eyes when he drank a mint julep, explained, "The sight of good lickah, suh, always makes my mouth watah, and I don't aim to have my drink diluted." The colonel, however, believes there is a time and place for everything. Observing his twenty-year-old son out on the veranda with a julep in one hand and the other hand around the waist of the belle of the county, he reflected, "That boy is squanderin' fifty per cent of his youth. He can drink when he gets old!"

A fugitive from Alcoholics Anonymous negotiated a job in a chinaware emporium, and succeeded in smashing an ornate vase before he had been there two hours. "Too bad," said the foreman, "but we'll have to deduct twenty per cent from your wages every week until the vase is paid for." "What did it cost?" asked the worker. "Five hundred bucks," said the foreman. The worker consoled himself, "My wife'll be pleased anyhow. This will be the first steady job I've had in ten years."

87

Hugh Ferry, of the Packard Motor Car Company, has a prescription for a hangover that he swears has never failed. "It's simplicity itself," says Ferry. "Just squeeze the juice from two quarts of Scotch."

A couple of vats at a beer brewery in Milwaukee were struck by lightning in a flash storm last summer. Not only were they undamaged, however, but experimentation proved that the beer within, instead of being spoiled, was actually improved in quality. The foreman smacked his lips over the unexpectedly fine flavor and wired the head of the outfit, "We believe this is the first case on record of a storm actually brewing."

An inquisitive guest asked Mrs. Cohalan: "What's in that bottle I saw in the kitchen?" Without looking up, Mrs. Cohalan replied, "Eight to one it's my husband Mike."

A long-suffering wife was about to berate her husband for staggering home at 3 A.M. "Before you begin," he warned her, "I want you to know I been sittin' up with a sick friend." "A likely story," mocked the wife. "What was his name?" The husband gave this problem deep thought, then announced triumphantly, "He was so sick he couldn't tell me."

I have it on the authority of expert William Feather that a Jeroboam of champagne contains 104 ounces of the bubbling vintage. A Split, furthermore, is a nip (6.4 ounces), a Fifth is a bottle (25.6 ounces), a Magnum is two bottles (52 ounces), a Rehoboam is six bottles (156 ounces), a Methuselah is eight bottles

(208 ounces), a Salmanazar is twelve bottles (312 ounces), a Balthazar is sixteen bottles (416 ounces), and a Nebuchadnezzar (wow!) is twenty bottles (520 ounces). Current quotation for a vintage Nebuchadnezzar is $375, plus $50 deposit for the bottle. First come, first served—and only two to a customer.

Old Colonel Archer, up from Kentucky, was describing his daily routine to a delighted group in Toots Shor's New York restaurant. "For breakfast," proclaimed the Colonel, "I ask only for a quart of bourbon, a pound of beefsteak, an' my ol' houn' dog." "What do you need the houn' dog for?" asked Toots. "The houn' dog," explained Colonel Archer, "eats the beefsteak."

J is for
JUDICIAL MATTERS

A couple of legal eagles in Reno, Nevada, write to say that while business never has been better, it docs grow somewhat boring to be handling the same kind of cases all the time. Is divorce, they ask plaintively, the *only* subject engaging the attention of the Law in America today?

At any rate, while waiting for the Truckee River to unfreeze last winter, so they could resume fishing for the gold wedding rings divorcees impulsively throw in when their decrees are granted, the impatient attorneys composed these pertinent couplets:

Mrs. Camp's bereft today. She always knew a shorter way.

No longer wed is Mrs. Thorne. She hogged the bathroom every morn.

Each week poor Sue found some new diet. Worse still, she made her husband try it.

Marriage, thought Jones, was sure and stable. But then he fed the dog at table.

She left him flat and deserted the scene. He ended each sentence with "See what I mean?"

Their marital break was grim and gory. She never would let him finish a story.

The Campbells are no longer lovers. She always woke up with no bed covers.

In Reno, John Doe is slowly reviving. He couldn't stand the backseat driving.

There is a successful lawyer in Hollywood whose name has been romantically linked with at least a dozen top-flight actresses from time to time. Tendered a fiftieth birthday party by his friends, the lawyer had to stand for a great deal of good-natured kidding. Always-reliable Georgie Jessel earned the biggest laugh by remarking, "Our esteemed guest of honor is going to be the lead-off man on any ball team I manage. He gets to first base so often!"

Grover Whalen is asking friends if they heard about the street cleaner who was dropped from the force because he couldn't keep his mind in the gutter. And Commissioner Cullman discloses the name invented by the police for kids picked up in disorderly houses: brothel sprouts.

A dairy in Iowa sued a minister for non-payment of a bill, but the case was thrown out when the minister's lawyer produced an analysis of the milk, and assured the court, "My client wanted that milk for drinking, not christening."

Chauncey Depew, addressing a graduating class at the Harvard Law School, reminded his audience, "Everything you learned here will go for naught if you forget this fundamental rule: when it becomes apparent in a case that somebody on your side is headed for jail, be sure it is your client!"

A showgirl with Dagmar-like accessories shot her boy-friend seven or eight times, and then cried her way through her trial—incidentally giving the jury ample close-ups of her abundant charms. The verdict was announced by the foreman in appropriately reverent tones: "We find the defendant breathtaking, entrancing, wholesome, lovable—and—oh, yes—not guilty."

A businessman was involved in a lawsuit that dragged on for years. One afternoon he told his attorney, "Frankly, I'm getting tired of all this litigation." "Nonsense," replied his lawyer. "I propose to fight this case down to your last nickel."

Judge Cohalan regarded the defendant at the bar severely and asked, "Have you ever been in trouble before?" "Coitn'ly not," was the vehement reply, "and the only t'ing dey're tryin' to pin on me dis time is robbin' me kid brudder's bank." "If I may be permitted to interrupt," spoke up the district attorney, "the prisoner neglected to explain that his kid brother is cashier of the First National Trust."

A very dignified judge was married to an estimable creature, who, unfortunately, drank a bit too much. At a party one afternoon he reproved her, "My dear, that's the fifth time you've gone up to the bar and asked for another highball. Doesn't it embarrass you?"

"Why should it?" she answered happily. "I just explain I'm getting them for you."

George Allen, the White House jester, avers that he but carries on the tradition of his father, who practiced law, politics, and diplomacy in Booneville, Mississippi. One day a magistrate forgot his cue and had the gall to decide a case *against* Allen, Senior. The latter waved a volume of Blackstone under the justice's nose to emphasize his outrage. "Sit down, Mr. Allen," thundered the judge. "I know the law." "Of course you do," purred Mr. Allen. "I just wanted to read this paragraph to you to show you what a damn fool Blackstone was."

I like the story that's come down from Sing Sing—of the condemned man walking to the electric chair, oblivious to the attendants surrounding him, reading a copy of *Quick!*

The warden of a big Western penitentiary, reports the Phoenix *Flame*, is conducting a thorough investigation of his office. While looking for some documents recently, he found one of the files had a cake in it. And Bernie Hart had a solution to offer the warden of the Michigan jail whose prisoners rioted and barricaded themselves in a cell block. "Offer them," suggested Bernie, "time and a half."

The most sensational trial of the year was in progress in Iceland, country of the midnight sun. The prosecuting attorney shook a bony finger in the face of the accused and thundered, "I ask you again, sir: where were you on the night of November 8 to March 16?"

The House Un-American Activities Committee has become used to evasive witnesses maintaining "I refuse to answer on the grounds that it might incriminate me," but one radio writer on the stand came up with a new one. Abel Green, of *Variety*, reports that this witness pondered over a question momentarily, then had a long whispered consultation with his lawyer, and finally answered, "I refuse to answer because I don't understand one damn word of my counsel's advice."

There's a man in Hollywood who is a great picture producer, but a child when it comes to high finance. His safe deposit box is the repository for just about every worthless oil stock floated in California. One day an acquaintance tried to sell him a whole gold mine at a "bargain" price. The producer promised to think it over and said "I'll call you." He did, too—about three days later— and declared, "My lawyer says I'm crazy but I've decided to buy that gold mine." "You're too late," answered the acquaintance bitterly. "I'm already in jail!"

K is for
THE KREMLIN

It appears that the question, "Who is going to inherit the mantle of Joe Stalin?" has been settled at last. On Georgi Malenkov's last birthday, the Soviet press accorded him so many hooplas that every comrade must have comprehended the general idea. They'll soon be getting "Won't You Be My Malenkovy Baby" as mujik in their ears.

Malenkov, son of a Cossack in the Urals, first hit the big time as Stalin's personal secretary in 1925, and showed that he was there to stay when he personally maneuvered the dismissal of the mighty Molotov's wife from her cushy post as Commissar of the Fish Industry.

"There are many, many fish in the sea," she had proclaimed. "Why aren't they on our citizens' tables?" demanded Malenkov.

American diplomats who attended Kremlin banquets in what now seems like the dim and distant days of World War II remember that Georgi Malenkov was always among those present, but invariably maintained a surly silence. Probably he knew even less English than his boss did.

At the Teheran conference, according to *Time* magazine, Joe Stalin's mastery of the English language was confined to two graphic sentences: "The toilet is over there," and "What the hell goes on here?"

A year later at the meeting in Yalta, he had added, "You said it" and "So what?"

A fugitive from Moscow managed to elude the border guards and presented himself to the American authorities in West Berlin. On his person were found a great variety of pills—and an enormous portrait of Stalin, printed on rubber and folded inside his belt. "The red pills are for sinus trouble," explained the Russian. "The green ones are for arthritis, the orange ones for toothaches, and the purple ones for indigestion." "Yeah, yeah," scoffed the examining sergeant, "but what's that picture of Joe Stalin for?" "That," said the Russian with great dignity, "is for homesickness."

At a party celebration in Leningrad, a guest discovered a piece of rubber tire in his stew. About to protest, he noticed the eye of a secret-police official fixed upon him, and managed a cheerful, "Well, everything is going according to our most optimistic calculations. Here we've been in power only thirty-five years, and already the automobile is replacing the horse!"

A Polish journalist, back in Warsaw after a brief journey to Moscow, was asked, "Is the Soviet really in such wonderful shape? Does the subway now extend sixty miles? Is every worker living in a new house with radio and air-conditioning? Is there a pile of atom bombs in the Kremlin? Are the farmers all happy and prosperous?" "Yes, yes," agreed the journalist. "All these things I saw with my own eyes." An old graybeard then asked, "And where is your companion Ignace? Why did he not return with you from Moscow?" "Alas," sighed the journalist. "Ignace is in a slave labor camp in Siberia. Unfortunately he did not seem to see all these things!"

Stalin called in his top "yes-men" one morning and boomed, "Boys, I've got a great idea! Let's liberate the Pribilof Islands from the suffocating grasp of those money-mad Wall Street bankers." One "yes-man" was a little slow with his usual enthusiastic endorsement. "I must point out," he quavered, "that there isn't a single human being on the Pribilof Islands—nothing but seals." That didn't stop Stalin. "Seals? People?" he roared. "After we get finished liberating them, who'll be able to tell the difference?"

At the finish line of a big bicycle race from Prague to Warsaw, a Polish lad watched eagerly until the last contestant pedaled by, then burst into tears. "Why weren't there any Russians in the race?" he sobbed. "I was hoping to get my bike back."

Sneaked out of Budapest is the story of the secret police agent who was ordered by his chief to learn whether a skeleton in the museum really was, as alleged, that of Attila, fifth-century chief-

tain of the savage Huns. The agent marched off with the skeleton
and returned forty-eight hours later with what was left of it—a
few splinters of bone. "It's Attila, all right," averred the agent.
"How did you confirm it?" asked the chief. The agent answered
proudly, "He confessed."

Commissar Malipoofsky journeyed from Moscow to Budapest
to see whether the Hungarian satellites were growing enough
potatoes to meet their quota. "Ah, Comrade," sighed his Hungarian deputy, "under the inspiration of the incomparable Stalin
our peasants are turning out a crop beyond our wildest dreams.
When they are harvested, our spuds, if put into a single pile, will
make a mighty mountain reaching to the feet of God." "Enough
of your hammy dramatics," said Commissar Malipoofsky sharply.
"Besides, you know perfectly well there isn't any God." The de-
flated deputy sighed, "There aren't any potatoes either."

John Cameron Swayze says that Stalin, Roosevelt, and Churchill were being driven in a staff car during their fateful Teheran
conference, when a cow blocked the road and refused to budge.
Neither Churchill's eloquence nor Roosevelt's charm was of any
avail. Stalin, however, merely whispered one phrase in the cow's
ear, and the animal bolted for the woods. When asked how he did
it, Stalin explained, "I just told her I was going to put her in a
collective farm."

The Soviet government recently hornswoggled a Swiss movie
manager into showing a hot propaganda film in his string of
theatres. It extolled Russian explorers in the frozen wastes of the
Arctic, showing thrilling polar-bear hunts, seal killing, and the
wonderful work of Russian ice-breaking ships and iceberg spot-

ters. One of the trimmest vessels bore a Russian name prominently on the bow. Swiss audiences watched in respectful silence, bursting into laughter only once. That was during a split-second shot, when a sign on the "Soviet" boat read very clearly, "United States Coast Guard."

Near the close of the Spanish Civil War the Russians sent a brigade of "volunteers" to be in on the fighting. Arrived in Madrid, the commissar in charge delivered this note to Loyalist headquarters: "Herewith two hundred wildly enthusiastic volunteers for your army. Please return the ropes."

An Irishman spent some time in the local pub listening to a broadcast of the latest news. Returning home he remarked to his wife, "They're saying it's Stalin who really has Korea." "Well," said the wife. "Bless the girl what gave it to him."

L is for
LITERARY LIFE

Literary history is studded with stories of great best sellers that were snubbed by anywhere from one to a dozen publishers before a more perspicacious—or lucky—one decided to take a chance. Cases in point are *The Four Horsemen of the Apocalypse*, Viña Delmar's *Bad Girl*, Ludwig's *Napoleon*, Mika Waltari's *The Egyptian*. An English publisher actually turned down Pearl Buck's *The Good Earth* twice! After he rejected it the first time, several other English houses followed suit, and the agent brought it back, insisting it belonged on his list. Again he said "no." The book sold almost a half million copies in Britain when another publisher accepted it.

The late S. S. McClure, pioneer magazine and book publisher, was waylaid on the way to his inner office one morning by a determined lady who demanded, "Did you keep your promise and read the manuscript I gave you?" To be rid of her, he answered, "I did. We can't use it." She appeared crestfallen and murmured, "I suppose the little verses at the beginning of each chapter detracted from the story. Maybe they should come out." "No, no," said the publisher suavely. "Those little verses add to the interest. I'd leave them in by all means."

"Mr. McClure," the lady answered triumphantly, "there *are* no little verses at the head of each chapter. You simply haven't read the manuscript as you said you would and I'm going to sit right

100

here until you do." McClure realized he was trapped, and with a sigh, sat down to skim through the manuscript as quickly as possible. He decided to accept it, however. The lady was Mrs. Ovid Butler Jameson of Indianapolis, determined to set her brother astride the high road to literary fame. Her brother's name was Booth Tarkington. The manuscript was *Monsieur Beaucaire.*

In 1939, Author Chard Powers Smith finished a novel and submitted it to Scribner's. The publishers approved of the book but were afraid his title would discourage customers. He consented to change it, and the book appeared in 1939 under the title of *The Artillery of Time.* Mr. Smith had occasion to doubt the wisdom of his move within a matter of weeks, for by purest chance John Steinbeck wrote a book with the very title Smith had been persuaded to discard—*The Grapes of Wrath.*

Publisher Richard Simon decided to include a half-dozen adhesives in a new juvenile called *Dr. Dan the Bandage Man,* and wired to a friend at the Johnson and Johnson Company, "Please ship two million band-aids immediately." Back came a telegram reading, "Band-aids on the way. What the hell happened to you?"

An important author arrived unannounced to see his publisher one Wednesday. "Sorry," said the receptionist, "but he's away for the week end." The author asked sarcastically, "Last week end or this week end?"

A man who had been a book salesman for twenty years decided there was more money in selling vacuum cleaners, and secured the local agency for a well-known brand. His very first prospect was a skeptical housewife who asked, "Are you sure that contraption will gather up every single bit of dirt?" "Lady," said the salesman earnestly, "I ran this cleaner lightly over a copy of *Lady Chatterley's Lover* yesterday, and when I was finished, it was Louisa Alcott's *Little Women!*"

Ed Laycock defines an intellectual snob as a man who won't speak to a beautiful girl on a train because he doesn't approve of the book she's reading. . . . William Butler Yeats characterized a literary movement as "two authors who live in the same city and hate each other." . . . Rebecca West described a pretentious society publisher as "every other inch a gentleman." . . . And bookmen who continually complain about the bad breaks they're getting might recall the words of Stephen Vincent Benét: "What some people call hard luck—well, we made New England out of it —that and codfish."

One of our most eloquent publishers, who will be disguised in this story under the name of Jones, was panting to move to his Westchester estate for the season, but found his plans stymied by his wife's inability to persuade a suitable butler to expose his precious carcass to the country air. "This servant problem is worse than ever," she complained. "Really! You'd think it was the Sahara we were asking them to come to, and not just twelve minutes from the White Plains station." "Tommyrot," declared Mr. Jones in his best *Life with Father* manner. "I will meet you at the agency tomorrow morning and show you how quickly the whole thing can be settled with the application of a modicum of common sense."

He was a few minutes late the next morning, and failing to note that the agency sported two entrances, one marked "employers," the other "employees," strode imperiously into the latter.

"Yes?" said the man who blocked his path. "What are you looking for?" "I am looking for Mrs. Jones," he announced. "She wants a butler." "Indeed she does," agreed the man, and propelled him in the direction of his reasonably puzzled wife. "Here, Mrs. Jones," he said, "is a man I know you'll like. I've placed him with some of our best clients, and he has never failed to give complete satisfaction."

The Joneses are still in Manhattan. Mrs. Jones is rounding out the staff by herself.

The early twenties evidently was a propitious period for the launching of new magazines in America. The *Reader's Digest* got under way in 1922, *Time's* first issue appeared in 1923, Mencken and Nathan's *American Mercury* made its bow in 1924, and the *New Yorker* began operations in 1925.

Mencken's rejection slips certainly were different from any others. Authors would get their brain children back with a printed slip reading, "Mr. Mencken has just entered a Trappist monastery in Kentucky and left strict orders that no mail was to be forwarded. The enclosed is returned therefore for your archives."

Two attractive young employees of a dashing midtown magazine publisher were discussing his merits. "He's so good looking," enthused one, "and he dresses so well!" The other amended happily, "So quickly, too!"

One of the many celebrities who dwell in Stamford, Connecticut, is editor Herbert Mayes, but his sumptuous home is so far from the town that servants are hard to find—and harder to keep. Mrs. Mayes finally latched on to a couple who seemed ideal, however, and after all arrangements had been concluded satisfactorily, led them in to meet Mayes in his study. Seeing the crowded bookshelves and piles of manuscripts, the butler was moved to inquire, "What's your line, sir?" Mayes answered, "I'm the editor of *Good Housekeeping Magazine.*" "*Good Housekeeping!*" gasped the butler, heading for the door. "Come on, Hilda, this is no place for us!"

Gordon MacRae says that, what with all the science fiction stories flooding the market, editors will soon have to change their formula to "Man gets girl; man loses girl; man builds girl."

A near-sighted publisher, walking along the beach at Province-town, Massachusetts, encountered a comely young lady who greeted him by name. Unable to recognize her without his glasses, the publisher stammered, "How nice to see you up here. How long are you staying?" "I've got to go home Sunday," she told him sadly. "What a pity," he remarked. "September is the best month on the Cape. Why don't you stay another week?" "I will if you'll let me," the girl said coyly.

The publisher examined her at close range and suddenly recognized her. It was his private secretary.

Editor Saxe Commins prevailed upon the beautiful new telephone operator to be his guest at luncheon, but when she returned she confided to a side-kick, "That's the last time I ever go to eat with an editor. He blue-penciled three fourths of my order!"

Charlie Marshall and Lew Miller, two of the most high powered and successful sales managers in publishing today, were, in

their salad days, rival book peddlers covering the same insignificant territory. Marshall remembers catching Miller one morning
dashing up and down a flight of stairs in their hotel as though his
life depended on his activities. "What on earth are you up to
now?" demanded Marshall. "Getting winded," explained Miller,
"so the first account I call on will think I'm breathless with excitement over our spring list."

Publisher Virgil Gentillin attended a cocktail party during a
recent librarians' convention. The discussion got around to the improvement of library service effected by more rigid requirements
and better training for aspiring librarians. One bright young thing
observed, "Do you know it takes five full years to make a librarian
now?" One visiting salesman, new in the racket, was appalled.
"I'm sorry, honey," he declared embarrassedly, "but I just haven't
got that much time."

In Tulsa, an oil magnate, enamored of his secretary's chassis
but appalled by her ignorance of literature, strove mightily to improve her I.Q. One morning she told him, "I took your advice. I
borrowed a book from the library last night." "Great," enthused
the magnate. "What was the name of it?" The secretary answered,
"Dun and Bradstreet's."

Stripper Lily St. Cyr reports that she's having trouble with the
books in her private library. "The minute I pick one up," she
pouts, "the jacket slips off."

A small come-on ad in a Paris newspaper recently brought rich
rewards to the bookseller who inserted it. "What every young girl

should know best before she weds," promised the ad. "Profusely illustrated. Explicit instructions. Sent in a plain envelope." Every eager soul who clipped the coupon received a very good cook book.

Relaxing by the swimming pool at La Quinta, in the California desert, mining executive Carl Loeb, Jr., remarked to Jerry Devine, producer of the successful radio series, "This Is Your F.B.I.," that he had written a book in his spare time. "What's the name of it?" asked Devine. Loeb glibly reeled off the title: "The Isothermal Transformation of Austenite in Molybdenum Steels." "I don't think I'll read it," decided Devine. "I'll wait for the picture."

A Chicago bookseller called his clerks into a huddle one morning and cautioned them, "I've ordered 300 copies of *What an Expectant Mother Should Know* and I'm counting on you boys to create a demand for them."

A Rolls-Royce stopped in front of a Madison Avenue bookshop the other evening, and the chauffeur announced rather sheepishly, "My lady wants a couple of new murder stories committed by *nice people*."

A religious bookshop near the State Capitol in Boston put on a big Bible sale recently and quite a number of customers were lured by this bit of versification on a card in the window:

> Holy Scripture, Writ Divine
> At a dollar forty-nine;
> Satan trembles when he sees
> Bibles sold as cheap as these.

A little girl was having a hard time in Brentano's Bookstore selecting a book to be given to her mother as a birthday gift. "Does she like fiction?" asked the clerk. The little girl shook her head. "Biography? History? Books on art? Humor?" The little girl continued to register disapproval. Finally the exasperated clerk demanded, "Well, what on earth *does* she like?" The little girl said, "Men."

M is for

MARTS OF TRADE

There exists a whole army of executives who never have learned the vital secret for keeping their private secretaries contented. Hell hath no fury like a secretary who nurses a grievance—be it real or imaginary. Take heed, therefore, of the results of a survey conducted by the personnel manager of a big woolen company to determine what kind of bosses irritate their secretaries most.

Here are the "winners"—and very much disputed champions:

1. The boss who keeps his secretary overtime without previous notice.

2. The boss who dawdles around until five P.M. and then begins the day's dictation.

3. The boss who refers to his secretary as his "stenographer" and makes bad jokes about her in front of visitors. Samples:

(A) "Better make twelve copies of this, Miss Winter, so we may be able to find one if we need it."

(B) "We're all in rather a hurry today, Miss Lyon, so how about taking this note down in longhand?"

(C) "It's quite true that we have done business with Gimbel's for decades, but we still do not address the president as 'Dear Gimmie.'"

4. The boss who marks up work that could be corrected, and slashes a line through a four-page letter because one word is incorrectly spelled.

108

5. The boss who interrupts his secretary during her lunch hour, if she has stayed to eat in her office.

6. The boss who hovers over her while she is typing a letter, pointing out errors before she has had a chance to notice them herself.

7. The boss who has seen too many Grade-B movies and cheap cartoons, and believes in the motto, "Hands Across the Knee."

8. The boss who never voluntarily says, "Gosh, your letters have been immaculate lately—and done so quickly, too," or "By the way, Miss Jones, isn't this your birthday?"

9. The boss who only gives a raise after the secretary has gone through countless humiliating sessions to wangle one. This type boss is usually the one who is most apt to flash a hefty bankroll continuously before his secretary's eyes.

10. The boss who regards his secretary as general errand girl for his entire family. She is expected to devote her lunch hour—particularly when it is raining heavily—to exchanging nylon stockings for his wife, picking up theatre tickets for his mother-in-law, and going to a repair shop clear across the city to find out why his brother's 1939 Buick is still out of commission.

Have you heard about the stunning young stenographer who left her coat in the office and took her boss to the cleaners?

Joe Gilligan's contracting firm was famous for its ability to slap together a whole block front of snazzy-looking (from the outside) ranch houses in less time than it took a builder of the old school to erect a chicken coop. One morning, however, a foreman rushed up to Gilligan and shouted, "We just removed the scaffolding from the three new houses on 'K' Street and they collapsed in a heap." Gilligan investigated, and turned on his foreman in a rage. "How often do I have to tell you ninnies," he bellowed, "never to remove the scaffolding till you've put up the wallpaper?"

Dave Garroway is acquainted with a Chicago merchant who was summoned suddenly to a big business powwow in New York. It was scheduled to last four days, and he had to grab a plane at the Cicero airport within the hour. Problem: how to contact his wife, who was on a shopping spree in the Loop? The merchant thought hard and suddenly came up with a brilliant idea. He ordered his secretary to cancel all of his wife's charge accounts. She called up in a rage twelve minutes later.

New high in absent-minded bosses is the bemused paper manufacturer who put the typewriter on his lap and started to unfasten the ribbon.

The third vice president of a downtown bank is a notorious ladies' man, despite his seventy years, and the girls in the organization make wide detours to escape his pinching forays. One morning last month, however, he barely looked up when movie star Anne Baxter ankled by. "Get a load of old J.W.!" marveled a member of the staff. "I'm afraid his eyes are on their last legs."

"But I thought . . ." said the secretary meekly.

"Don't think," barked the industrialist. "That's not what I pay you for. Take down what I dictate and then type the letters. Is that quite clear? Now take this."

That afternoon, his secretary planked this letter on his desk for signature:

"Dear Smythe: The idiot spells it with an 'E'. Thinks it's aristocratic. His old man was a plumber. With regard to your letter of —look it up. Anybody who can read that handwriting deserves a medal. You ask the cost of replacing worn parts in the machinery at your plant. Our experts figure—hey, Joe, what was the estimate on that Smythe job? Two thousand? Okay—our experts figure that three thousand dollars is our rock-bottom price. The extra thousand is for that damn 'E' he sticks on his name. Trusting to receive your esteemed order, etc., etc., etc. There, that's done and you better get off my lap before my partner walks in on us."

Three old friends, all unemployed, set out together one morning to seek jobs. That evening, the wife of the eldest said, "Well, Joe, what luck today?" "Sam struck it rich anyhow," said Joe. "On his first call, a fellow took him up to a desk marked 'Treasurer' and told him he was now treasurer of the corporation." "What about Bill?" asked the wife. "Bill got a break, too," answered Joe. "A man showed him a room labeled 'Vice-president' and that's the job they gave him." "Wonderful," said the wife, "but what happened to you?" "Congratulate me, mama," said Joe quizzically. "At last, I'm a gentleman."

Stanley McMichael, author of *How to Make Money in Real Estate*, knows an operator who owned a loft building, a marble yard with dock privileges, a factory site and a summer garden, all of which he proposed to swap with another man who owned a row of tenements, a small subdivision, an abandoned lime kiln and a farm. "He assumes a $20,000 mortgage on the loft building," explained the first man to his wife, "and I take over a second mortgage on the subdivision. Get me?" "I guess so," responded the wife wearily, "but if you've got all the details so cleverly worked out, what's holding up the deal?" "I sign nothing," he declared firmly, "till he gives me four dollars in cash!"

The young man was obviously embarrassed. He explained haltingly, "I'm supposed to bring home either a casserole or camisole. I can't remember which." "That dilemma is easily resolved," chuckled the erudite storekeeper. "Is the chicken dead or alive?"

Drew Pearson recently wowed his audience at the Detroit Athletic Club with another story of a man who visited a Washington department store to buy a brassiere for his wife. "What kind do you want?" demanded the salesgirl. "We have the Stalin, the Salvation Army, and the Drew Pearson." Noting Pearson's utter mystification, she condescended to explain, "The Stalin model uplifts the masses. The Salvation Army supports the fallen. And the Drew Pearson make mountains out of molehills."

Andrew Carnegie once was showing a delegation through his plant when he stopped to talk to a stooped, gray-haired employee. "Let's see, Wilson," he said. "How many years exactly is it that you've been with me now?"

"Thirty-nine, sir," beamed Wilson. "And may I add that in that entire time I made only one trifling mistake?" "Good work," grunted Mr. Carnegie, "but from now on, please be more careful."

From Philadelphia comes the story of two suspender salesmen who were boasting of their products. "Five army mules pulled on either end of a pair of our braces," proclaimed one, "and they couldn't make them break."

"Paghh!" scoffed the other. "Yesterday I was rushing to catch a train at Penn Station in New York, and my suspenders got caught in a pillar on the platform. I made my train all right, but when the conductor opened the door in Philadelphia, those darn suspenders of ours snapped me right back to New York!"

A couple of furriers had had an unusually successful season and the senior partner flew down to Miami Beach for a well-earned vacation. He had been there two days when his partner in New York called him long distance to splutter, "Our safe has been robbed! $50,000 is missing!" The senior partner calmly replied, "Now, Joe, that's going entirely too far. You put $45,000 right back in the safe."

Landlord Vogel slid an overdue rent bill under the door of a dilatory Broadway character, who promptly slid it out again. Twice more Vogel pushed it back into the room—and twice more it came back. Vogel straightened up, sighed deeply, and reflected, "I guess I'll have to fix his window after all. There's certainly a powerful draught in here."

A wholesale outfit in New York has so many customers it's able to classify them according to their habits of speaking. To wit:

Musical buyer: I'll make a *note* of it.
Animal buyer: I'll *bear* your *lion* in mind.
Marine buyer: I'll be in to *sea* you when you have a *sail*.
Russian buyer: I'll take *one uv ich*.
Romantic buyer: I *love* everything you've shown me—but. . . .
Blanket buyer: I want you to *cover* me.
Barber buyer: Can't you *shave* your price a bit?
Ideal buyer (Imaginary): I'll take everything!

A young salesman in a dress manufacturer's office was assigned the task of entertaining a very important out-of-town buyer. The sky was the limit, and the boss gave him 200 smackeroos for an evening's fun and relaxation. The buyer, however, proved to be a very difficult hombre. He had seen *Guys and Dolls* eight times—"Everybody takes me to see *Guys and Dolls*"—and *Pal Joey* five times. He was bored with the show at the Copa and every other night club in town. Every suggestion the salesman made bounced back in his teeth. Finally, in desperation, he turned to the buyer and said, "I've got no more suggestions to make. Suppose *you* tell *me* what you'd like to do." Answered the buyer, "What I'd really like to do is visit a high-class sporting house."

The next day, the salesman reported for work and handed over to the boss $190 out of the $200 he had been given. His employer was flabbergasted and asked how come? "Well," said the salesman, "Mr. X wanted only one thing—to go to a high-class sporting house. So I took him to Abercrombie & Fitch, but it was closed."

Samson, notes Copywriting Genius Milton Biow, really had the right idea about advertising. He took two columns and brought down the house.

One of the kids at Deerfield Academy asked Washington corre-
spondent Bert Andrews about his early days in the journalistic
profession. Andrews knitted his brows, and pondered, "I believe
I got my first scoop when I was four years old, and yes—it was
vanilla."

At an alumni meeting of Public School 14, a member of the
class of 1910, now balding and affluent, reminisced, "Do you fellows remember a skinny little shaver named Hughes from our
class? His family was poor as church mice, but he had an instinc-
tive business sense, and we all just knew he'd make the grade. I
ran into Hughes the other day. When he got out of the Army in
World War I, he bought himself an old push-cart and began buying and selling old bones, bottles, and rags. And what do you
think Hughes is worth today?" Some guessed $100,000, some a
million. "You're all wrong," chuckled the alumnus. "Hughes isn't
worth a Confederate nickel. In fact, he never even paid for the
push-cart."

One of the slickest operators in the garment district, relates
Harry Hershfield, always dated his checks ahead. When he passed
away, creditors erected a tombstone over his grave. It read, "Here
lies Gabriel Gluntz. Died November 10, as of February first."

A tourist bought a bolt of beautiful British cloth in the Bahamas
and presented it to his Fifth Avenue tailor, asking, "Is there
enough material here for you to make me a suit?" "No," said the
tailor. The disappointed tourist headed for home, and passed a

tiny sidestreet tailoring shop en route. "No harm to try again," he thought, and sure enough, the second tailor was confident he could make him a very adequate suit from the material available.

He was true to his word, and a fortnight later turned out a garment that fitted the tourist like a glove. Just as the latter was reaching for his pocket book, however, the tailor's five-year-old son ran into the shop, garbed in a suit so obviously cut from the tourist's own material, the tailor didn't even attempt to alibi. "Yes, I made a suit for my boy from the goods left over," he said placatingly. "There wasn't enough to be of any use to you anyhow!" At that moment the tourist bethought himself of Tailor Number One. Angrily charging into that worthy's establishment he cried, "Remember telling me I didn't have enough material for a suit? A competitor down the block not only made me a very fine one, but had enough cloth left over to make a suit for his five-year-old son!" "So what?" scoffed Tailor Number One. "*My* son is eighteen!"

Delferd Clark, one of the directors of the Ford Foundation, describes the visit of a delegation to the home offices of one of the country's biggest manufacturers of business machinery. The head of the firm marched the visiting group from one mechanical marvel to another, and once the ground floor had been covered, led the way to the elevator. One of the other occupants of the elevator was a beautiful young blonde. Halfway to the second floor, the blonde suddenly jumped two feet in the air, and squealed, "Yipes!" The leader of the delegation nodded his head and said with great satisfaction, "I'm certainly glad to note that at least *one* thing in this building is still done by hand!"

N is for a
NEW PARLOR GAME

Bright young boys and girls in the literary set like radio tycoon Bill Paley, composer Harold Rome, Russell Austin, Gross-Vater Arthur Kober, and Quiz Kids originator Lou Cowan, have been knocking themselves out with a new parlor game called "In the Name Of." It demands the merest smattering of knowledge of great personalities in history and the arts plus a knack for making —and deciphering—atrocious puns. You can understand why *I* like it!

For example, a German plutocrat is showing his country estate to a friend. The friend declares "Most beautiful lawn and gardens I ever saw!" The German shrugs it off in the name of an English author (also, to make it easier, in the name of a popular brand of cigarettes) with "Ach, it's Chesterfield!" (Just a field). Another example: two Englishmen hail each other in the name of a famous French painter. Answer: Watteau (What, ho!). Everything clear? The solutions to all that follow will be found at the end of this section—but before you look there, try to solve them yourself.

1. The drama critic of a big New York daily fell ill on the eve of an important play's debut. His wife went to review it in his stead. The author of the play awaited her verdict in a fever of anxiety, finally called a friend on the paper.

"What did she say?" he implored. The friend answered in the name of an Indian lady who is much in the news.

2. A transcontinental express train was wrecked in the desert. The life of the engineer (a Frenchman) was spared, and he was speedily summoned by a board of inquiry. "In your opinion," he was asked, "what caused this catastrophe?"

"Eet is very seemple," he said, and explained in the name of a nineteenth-century painter, especially popular in America today.

3. Mrs. Jones thought the movers had taken everything out of her home but suddenly discovered they had overlooked a valuable vase. She told her Chinese houseboy, "The moving men must take this vase with them." "Lady too late," sighed the houseboy.

"Why?" asked the lady. The houseboy explained in the name of a Dutch painter who once cut off his ear.

4. Three fellows named Tom, Fred, and Ces decided to enact the famous jousting scene in *Don Quixote*. "I'll play the title role," proposed Tom, "Fred can portray Sancho Panza, and——."

5. A Montreal-bound lady woke up in her berth to find the temperature of the car down to 20°. Ringing for the attendant, she announced indignantly, "I'm ——."

6. A lady was playing Christmas songs at the piano, when a page of her songbook fluttered to the floor.

Her daughter pointed out what had happened in the name of the author of one of the world's best known children's classics.

7. A barker on a carnival midway beckoned a sweet young thing and enticed her with, "Wanna win a crisp new twenty-dollar bill, girlie? All ya gotta do is throw one of these rings over that cane in the back of the booth."

The sweet young thing sought further information in the name of another great Dutch painter.

8. A dairy farmer's whole livelihood was endangered when his prize cow suddenly went dry. Anxiously he summoned the most distinguished vet in the country—a foreigner whose skill had won him a dozen degrees.

The vet examined the ailing animal carefully, then rose and patted the worried farmer on the back, reassuring him in the name of a distinguished modern Russian composer.

ANSWERS: 1. Madame Pandit. 2. Toulouse-Lautrec (Too loose le track). 3. Van Gogh. 4. Cecil B. De Mille. 5. Cole Porter. 6. Lewis Carroll (Loose carol). 7. Vermeer (From here?). 8. Shostakovich ("Just a cow itch").

Let's see you do better!

O is for

OUR FOUR-LEGGED FRIENDS

Including Shaggy Dogs

A report from the jungle, difficult to track down but believed to emanate from horses considered reliable, has it that the animal world was anything but pleased when Mr. Aesop began composing his beastly fables. D. B. Wyndham, in fact, avers that one morning a grape-hating fox who felt that he had been libeled sneaked up behind Mr. Aesop and bit a substantial piece out of his hide. "Now go home and write that up," he sneered.

With unrest of this sort pervading the forest primeval, a proud and domineering lion decided it was time he checked the loyalty of his constituents. Collaring a stray antelope, he demanded, "Who is the king of the animal world?" The antelope, no fool he, hastily answered, "You, oh mighty lion." The lion roared his satisfaction and skulked along until he encountered a wise old chimpanzee. "Who is the king of the animal world?" snarled the lion who, as you can see, had something of a one-track mind. "You, of course," soothed the chimp. "What monk doesn't know a thing like that?" The lion was a happy beast until he ran into a ponderous and ill-tempered elephant. Again he demanded, "Who is the king of the elephant world?" By way of reply, the pachyderm promptly wrapped him up in his trunk, whirled him aloft four or five times, and deposited him in a bramble bush twenty feet away. Regaining his feet with difficulty, the bruised lion observed plaintively, "Just because you don't know the answer, you don't have to lose your temper!"

120

A persnickety mule on a Southern plantation, more obstreperous even than his usual wont, kicked over an outhouse and considerable section of back fence, and was roundly beaten for his pains. A poodle seized the occasion to point a moral to her pups. "Children," she said, "let that jackass be a warning to you against the habit of kicking. Just you notice how the better he does it the more unpopular he gets." Play-agent Monica McCall's poodle, incidentally, recently started chewing up a college dictionary. Miss McCall took the words right out of his mouth.

Blanche Rizzardi, of Minersville, Pa., writes about the frustrated glow-worm who tried to strike up a conversation with the lighted end of a cigarette. Doris Warner, of the Hollywood Solarium, knows a porcupine who got into even worse trouble. He's so near-sighted that he made love to a cactus plant. Ray Bowden, of Gloucester, Massachusetts, overheard a little germ on the edge of a milking pail comment sadly to another little germ, "Our relations seem to be getting strained."

A dog and a cat became embroiled in a street-corner fight, and a big crowd gathered to watch. One unruly spectator suddenly whipped a gun out of his pocket and shot the dog. A policeman heard the report and came running on the double. The killer threw his gun to the ground and appealed to the crowd, "Don't say a word to the cop. He'll think the cat did it!" A lady in Wichita loved goldfish so passionately that she kept her tub in the bathroom filled to the brim with them. "But what happens when you take a bath?" asked a friend. "What do you do with the goldfish?" The lady blushed modestly and explained, "I just blindfold them."

A hillbilly, notes Mrs. Arthur Magners, of Reading, Pennsylvania, spied a parrot atop a barn roof, and attracted by its plumage, decided to capture it for a pet. He climbed up to the rooftop and made a grab, but the parrot moved out of his range, ruffled his feathers, and snapped, "What do you think you're doing, brother?" The hillbilly tipped his hat and apologized, "Beg pardon, sir. I thought you were a bird."

A health crank, partial to yogurt and such like, felt a sudden craving for a plate of clam chowder, and what with it being a Friday, decided to indulge himself. He took the precaution, however, of presenting the waiter with two huge vitamin pills, and instructed him to dissolve them in the chowder before serving. When a half hour went by without a sign of chowder, the health crank collared the waiter and hollered, "Why am I receiving no service around here?" "You'll get your chowder, sir," soothed the waiter, "the minute we can get the clams to lie down."

A city feller who doesn't know the front end of a goat from a magnolia bush was watching his week-end host's daughter milking her cow when a farm hand hollered, "Cheese it, here comes the bull!"

The city feller vaulted a fence for safety, but noted to his surprise that the girl never budged from her stool. Furthermore, the bull brought up abruptly, snorted almost apologetically and meekly retreated to his enclosure. "Weren't you petrified?" demanded the guest.

"Not me," said the daughter, "but I reckon the bull was. This here cow's his mother-in-law."

Some months ago, a collection of wealthy ornithologists in New Jersey triumphantly announced that they had tracked down the nesting grounds of a very elusive bird named the bristle-thighed curlew. This name, for some reason, caused numerous readers to begin inventing ridiculous species of non-existent birds, the craziest of which were duly listed in *Tide*, the advertisers' bible. Examples: the tufted dowager, red-eyed crosspatch, lesser stench, double-breasted seersucker, morning peewee, electric crane, week-end bat, vested interest, bleary-eyed hangover, and extra-marital lark.

A mother hen, experiencing difficulty in keeping a headstrong chick in line, finally declared, "If your pa could see you now, he'd turn over in his gravy."

A hunter with a big gun, goes a current legend, met up with a bear that had no gun at all. But the bear had claws—and wit— and refused to concede defeat. He asked the hunter, "What are you looking for?" "A fine fur coat," said the hunter. "Me, I'm looking for breakfast," declared the bear. "What do you say to coming round to my nice warm den and talking over our prospects?"

So they went to the den and worked out a satisfactory compromise. The bear, emerging solo from the den, had enjoyed a splendid breakfast, and the hunter was wrapped up in a fine fur coat.

Farmer Ekhamer owned a very tough ram, but discovered that music soothed its savage breast. Headed for town one day, Ekhamer reminded his son, "If that animal gets rambunctious just put a record on the Victrola." When he returned home he discovered that the ram had plunged against a stone wall and committed suicide. "Did you play music like I told you?" he demanded of the son. "I sure did," said the boy, "but the record I chose seemed to drive him crazy. It was Frank Sinatra singing, 'There'll Never be Another Ewe.'"

Patricia Richardson's dog, "Faun," had an aggravating habit of curling himself up in his mistress' favorite easy chair, and feigning sleep when she attempted to dislodge him. Next door there resided a cat whom Faun abhorred, however, and Miss R. learned that by going to the window and crying "Here comes that cat,"

Faun could be persuaded to vacate the chair and vanish from sight without further ado. She had worked this dodge effectively on several occasions when, one afternoon, she sat dozing in her chair. Faun walked in, studied her with his head on one side, suddenly bounded to the door and began barking furiously. The aroused Miss Richardson rushed to investigate. The street was absolutely empty. When she returned, Faun was curled up blissfully, his eyes closed, in the easy chair.

The cat is one reasonably domesticated animal that most people find impossible to take or leave casually. The reactions of my own friends, for instance, range from Authoress Leonora Hornblow, who verges on hysteria at mere sight of a cat to Authoress Bernardine Kielty, who considers a dinner incomplete unless her Siamese Suki drops at least once from some lofty perch into the ragout. John Beecroft, who picks books for the Literary Guild, has so many cats around the house that it's a lucky visitor who escapes without hurt felines. James Mason, the picture star, goes him about twenty better.

Fred Allen, bosom friend of the Masons, was dining one evening at the home of Mary and Jack Benny. "You're sitting at my usual place at the table," Mary informed him, "so will you please fish under your chair for the buzzer to summon the butler? Then tell me what the Masons do with all those cats around the house." "For one thing," answered Allen gravely, "they never have to hunt for a buzzer. They just step on one of the cats."

The old comedy team of Moran and Mack had a cat routine that always won a solid laugh. Moran claimed that he owned fifteen cats, and therefore drilled fifteen holes in his dining room door so he could get rid of them when he desired. "But one hole would be enough," Mack pointed out. "The cats could exit one by one." "Nothing doing," concluded Moran firmly. "When I say 'scat' I mean 'scat.'"

A pedigreed and very expensive cat was shipped from Philadelphia by overnight truck to a purchaser in New York. The

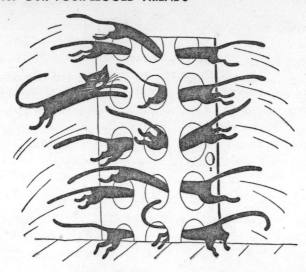

driver later confessed to Michael Gross, the poster artist, that while he was bumping along the cobblestones on Eleventh Avenue, the jarring loosened the cage in which the cat was confined. With one mighty leap he was off, high-tailing it up the avenue. Shouts of onlookers alerted the driver, who instituted an intensive cat-hunt, but to no avail.

All he found was a scurvy-looking scavenger in an alley. Figuring that all was lost anyhow, he collared the unsavory specimen, shoved him into the cage, and delivered him to the purchaser. Here's the pay-off. To this day the purchaser, evidently highly satisfied with his alley cat, has never registered a single word of protest!

The late Al Jolson had a cat which he told his friends was worth $5000. Came the day when he decided to sell the animal, and the skeptical friends waited eagerly for him to return from the pet shop and disclose the selling price. "Did you get the $5000?" they jeered. "Certainly," answered Al. "Did you think I was kidding you?" "Show us the dough," demanded the friends. "Well," admitted Al, "this pet shop fellow happened to be a little short of cash so he gave me these two $2500 dogs instead."

An embittered government worker in Washington tells the story of two lions who escaped from the zoo and didn't meet again for three months. One was fat, the other nothing but skin and bones. The skinny one said, "I've never seen you looking so well fed. How on earth have you managed?" The fat one said casually, "I've been holing up at the Pentagon Building, eating a general or admiral a day. So far nobody's noticed it."

From Montana comes a delectable new shaggy dog story. Seems an old prospector was reminiscing for some Eastern tenderfoots. "There I was," he asserted, "trapped in a narrow canyon, with a big grizzly twenty yards away behind a tree. Only way I could hit the critter was to ricochet a bullet off the high canyon wall on my right. Now I'm a champion shot, as you probably know. I just gauged my windage, calculated the lead of the barrel and the rate of twist, the hardness of the bullet and the angle of yaw it would have after being smacked out of shape against the canyon wall, and I judged my chances of nailing that bear were about 80–20. A one-rail bank shot. A controlled ricochet. So I took aim and fired."

The prospector paused. One of the tenderfeet asked softly, "Did you hit him?"

"Nope," answered the old man. "I missed the wall."

An outstanding social event of the Sewickley, Pennsylvania, season was the hunt tea given by Mr. and Mrs. Joseph Purslove, Jr., to fete "widows, widowers, and orphans of the hunt." The general idea, read the invitation, was to recognize the plight of unfortunates to whom "brush means Fuller, giving tongue is wife's noises, a good fencer parries thrusts with a rapier, a rising scent is inflation, a waving stern is a sinking ship, whip means prunes, and drawing a covert is caused by a sudden drop in the temperature at night."

Ted Weeks, editor of the *Atlantic Monthly*, brought home from England an essay by a ten-year-old that he swears is the genuine article, although I have a vague notion I read it somewhere before. Can any reader supply further details? The piece is called "A Bird and a Beast," and it reads as follows:

The bird that I am going to write about is the Owl. The Owl cannot see at all by day and at night is as blind as a bat.

I do not know much about the Owl, so I will go on to the beast which I am going to choose. It is the Cow. The Cow is a mammal. It has six sides—right, left, and upper and below. At the back it has a tail on which hangs a brush. With this it send the flies away so that they do not fall into the milk. The head is for the purpose of growing horns and so that the mouth can go somewhere. The horns are to butt with, and the mouth is to moo with. Under the cow hangs the milk. It is arranged for milking. When people milk, the milk comes and there is never an end to the supply. How the cow does it I have not yet realized, but it makes more and more.

The cow has a fine sense of smell; one can smell it far away. This is the reason for the fresh air in the country.

The man cow is called an ox. It is not a mammal. The cow does not eat much, but what it eats it eats twice, so that it gets enough. When it is hungry it moos, and when it says nothing it is because its inside is all full up with grass.

Ted Dealey, of the Dallas *News*, tells the story of the farmer whose plan to mate his mare and the prize stallion of the county was frustrated by the stallion's untimely demise. The farmer led up a zebra from the zoo as the likeliest substitute he could find, but the mare indicated plainly "No soap." "I went to a lot of trouble to get this zebra," the farmer complained to the mare, "and besides, he has an exceptional pedigree, so what are you getting so hoity-toity about?" The mare lowered her eyes bashfully and replied, "Who's getting hoity-toity? I'm just waiting for him to take off his pajamas."

P is for the

PUN-AMERICAN CONFERENCE

There are no two ways about puns. You either like them or you don't. If you don't, this section is not for you. If you do, gather round for some of the worst of the year. And to be successful, a pun really must be bad. It must make the listener groan dismally, shake his head disapprovingly, and stagger off to the next room where, no doubt, he promptly repeats it as his own.

Until the Pun-American Conference really got into the groove in my Cerf Board column in *This Week Magazine*, I never realized how many folks were in a punsive mood these days. Already three secretaries have been stricken with appundicitis merely from opening the mail.

One who may never recover at all drew a stunner that came all the way from Allan Bosworth, now a captain with the Atlantic fleet. It concerned a beauty-shop proprietor whose hired hands were out on strike. He didn't mind being picketed as long as the girls were pulchritudinous but rebelled when he discovered that the babe who was parading back and forth in front of his entrance had been a victim of smallpox.

He called union headquarters and roared, "This time you're going too far. My picket has been pocked!"

Gypsy Rose Lee was playing a sketch in an old musical revue that called for the property man to ring a deep gong off stage at a certain point in the proceedings. One day the property man mis-

placed his gong, and in desperation, shook a little dinner bell he
found on the shelf. The unexpected, silvery tinkle caused Miss
Lee to burst out laughing, and the punch line of the sketch was
lost as a consequence.

When she returned to the wings, she demanded that the property man be fired forthwith. The stage manager, who had been
out having a beer while the act was in progress, asked the cause
of her ire. Gypsy explained, "He ain't done right by our knell."

Bob Campbell, of Westwood, hired three adjoining rooms at
the Beverly Hills Hotel for a business powwow, and found a
bottle of bitters in one of them. He tried to turn the bottle over to
Manager Hernando Courtright, but the latter said, "Nay, nay.
You've got to take the bitters with the suite." . . . Mrs. Charles
Lederer avers that Ethel Barrymore, detected trimming her lawn
with a nail scissors, explained her behavior with a well-modulated
"That's all there is; there isn't any mower." . . . A final dispatch
from our Hollywood chapter expresses regret that Abraham
Lincoln never met Florenz Ziegfeld. Frank Larkin daydreams, "I
can see the headline now: Abe and Flo."

At a dinner given by the Book-of-the-Month Club to honor
Dorothy Canfield Fisher, she dropped a paper on the floor. Chris-
topher Morley stooped to retrieve it for her, but a certain middle-
age spread impeded his progress. Clifton Fadiman observed,
"Chris is still as gallant as when Dorothy was a gal, but not as
buoyant as when he was a boy."

Another double pun was perpetrated by a guest of a San Francisco hostelry. Several chess players had formed the habit of
staging daily contests in the lobby, and a crowd of kibitzers

gathered to watch them. The manager, noting that they produced no revenue for the hotel, ordered them cleared out one afternoon.

At the height of the resultant hullabaloo, a lady asked, "What's happened?" That's when the guest contributed his classic: "It's nothing, ma'am: just the manager pulling his chess nuts out of the foyer."

Irving Titsworth called on Judge Brown one evening during the dinner hour. "I'm sorry," the maid told him firmly, "but His Honor is at steak." . . . A hermit in an obsolete jalopy was apprehended driving in Pomona, California, at 70 miles an hour. The charge, of course, was recluse driving . . . Bess Vaughan says the trouble with her new nylons is that they're sheer today and torn tomorrow.

Near the conclusion of World War II, recalls John Pericola, a jeepload of Tito's soldiers was speeding along a sketchy, winding road in the Yugoslavian mountain country. Rounding a curve at high speed, the jeep plowed into an oxcart filled with natives. After the crash, they had the devil's own time separating the jeep from the Croats. . . . Mike Connolly knows why the population of Italy is soaring. Tony's Home Permanent.

America lost one of its first-rate humorists when Fred Taylor, known to millions as "Colonel Stoopnagle," died in Boston. Some of his screwball "inventions" were round dice for people who preferred marbles; red, white and blue starch to keep American flags waving when there was no wind; and the "tates," a compass that invariably pointed in the wrong direction. "In this manner," explained the Colonel, "he who has a tates is lost." Stoop also introduced an alarm clock with half a bell to wake only one person in a room, and a goldfish bowl surrounded by postcards so the fish would think they were going somewhere.

In the boundless ocean, notes Vera Lawrence, a father drop and a mother drop determined to teach their young offspring how to be a responsible part of the sea. After a month of intensive training the father drop observed his son's antics with satisfaction.

He then announced to the mother drop, "I do believe we've taught Junior everything he has to know. I hereby declare him fit to be tide."

In Paris, John Woodburn even negotiated a pun in French. He noticed that a lady's petticoat had slipped and was collecting dust as she promenaded down the Rue de la Paix.

Tapping her on the shoulder he pointed out, "Mademoiselle, your *quelque chose*."

Richard Anderson's next-door neighbor has triplets, and since nobody can tell them apart, they're known simply as "A," "B" and "C." The three boys were having trouble learning to back up on their birthday tricycles. After many bumps and bruises, "A" finally mastered the reverse pedaling, and his mother exclaimed happily, "Ah, my 'A' can back!" . . . Mr. Anderson will kindly stand in the corner with Margaret Davis who writes from Monterey, California, about an elderly lady who hesitated at a busy intersection.

A gentleman, noting her confusion, inquired, "Have you vertigo, madam?" She replied, "Yes, a mile."

At one Puntagon session, first prize went by default—and de fault was that of Major Al Furst, of Norfolk (that Furst family of Virginia you've been hearing about).

Major Furst's atrocity concerns two German lads named Hans and Fritz—who else?—who were proceeding gingerly along a narrow mountain ridge with their mother in tow. Below them was a drop of five thousand feet.

Fritz, who was in the lead, suddenly discovered that his mother had disappeared. So he called back to his brother, "Look, Hans: no mom."

When *Guys and Dolls* was being organized, an aspirant for a minor singing role failed to meet the requirements of composer Frank Loesser (pronounced Lesser) and his wife, Lynn.

The aspirant skulked into the night, muttering angrily, "I owe my predicament to the evil of two Loessers."

A poker-loving spiritualist wanted another player for a Saturday-night session and summoned the ghost of a departed companion. The ghost was delighted to sit in on the game, and on the very first hand drew five beautiful hearts. He bet his stack.

Unfortunately, one of the flesh-and-blood players had a pat full house and raked in the pot—just one more time when the spirit was willing but the flush was weak.

Sigmund Spaeth insists that you hear about the Peruvian prince who fished a beautiful maiden out of an enchanted lake and made her his before the Inca was even dry. . . . In baseball-mad Chicago, Carl Kroch, endeavoring to teach his beautiful wife German, asked, "Was sagst du?" She answered, "They lost, 7 to 1." . . . Matt Rae knows a dentist who was summoned by Poet Carl

Sandburg to alleviate a toothache. After some investigation he whispered to an assistant, "My reputation is made! I've discovered Carl's bad Caverns."

As Noah remarked while the animals were boarding the Ark, "Now I herd everything."

Q is for

QUALITY FOLK
Get Rich and Worry!

Life among the high and flighty is very luxurious and glittering, but with every million in the bank come new dilemmas and distractions that never bother ordinary folk at all. Even the children of the rich can't escape them—for all their silver spoons and golden high chairs.

The seven-year-old daughter of a Hollywood millionaire, for instance, was a guest at a birthday party where all the other kids were gobbling ice cream with gusto. She, however, sought out the birthday child's mother and asked severely, "May I feel quite sure that this is Harmon's Non-Allergic Ice Cream?"

Taxes, of course, are a perpetual thorn in the side of the wealthy. A member of the class of '19 at Princeton had a hard time persuading two of his wealthiest classmates to join him in promoting a new corporation that he hoped would earn a fortune. Both agreed the enterprise looked good, but pointed out that, because of taxes, it meant nothing more to them than additional headaches.

"I know," agreed the promoter, "but you two are my oldest friends, and I wouldn't feel right about going into this deal without you."

"All right," agreed the wealthier of the two reluctantly, "but one thing must be distinctly understood in advance. If we make the money you predict—you have to keep it."

As though a new house owner in the suburbs hasn't enough worries, with mortgages, furnishings, landscaping, and water supply to look after, he's also faced with the problem of finding a clever and appropriate name for the estate. Brilliant gems of wit like "Bankruptcy Court," "So-and-so's Folly," and "Tottering-on-the-Brink" usually are discarded in the nick of time, and when the shiny new station wagon makes its first trip to the village, a time-honored and safe stand-by like "The Willows," "River View," or "Gooseberry Hill" is painted on its side.

A few die-hards, however, have insisted on house names that are unique. Alexander Woollcott dubbed his place "Wit's End." A publisher selected "Galleys West." Thyra Samter Winslow, upon acquiring the smallest house in Greenwich Village, aptly named it "Writer's Cramp." Another author chose "The Palazzo Thickens."

The home of Westchester's most gracious and indefatigable hostess is known as "Sans Repos." An old geometry professor at Williams retired to a manse appropriately titled "After Math." A pillar of Alcoholics Anonymous selected "Chez When." A barrister converted a hayloft into a modernistic villa and christened it "Barn Yesterday." John Barrymore referred to his first country seat as "Barrymore's Bluff." The publisher of a successful line of 25-cent books named his hacienda "The Quarters." And they say that Paul Hoffman, appalled at the number of petitioners seeking largesse from the Ford Foundation he heads, is toying with re-naming his estate "Itching Palms."

The secretaries of mighty industrialists are not necessarily brilliant—but I've noticed they're always beautiful. A brand-new one was summoned by Banker Paul Warburg one morning and told, "My phone seems to be out of order. Please ask the phone company to get somebody over here to fix it." "Who shall I ask for?" inquired the secretary. "The president," suggested Warburg, sarcastically.

An hour later, a workman in overalls, toting a repair kit, barged into Warburg's office without knocking and emptied his tools on the floor with a crash. Warburg's anger was appeased when he got a good look at the impolite workman. It was his good friend, Walter Gifford, then head of the Board of American Telephone and Telegraph Company.

At a glittering opening night on Broadway appeared a famous oil tycoon, on his arm a magnificently proportioned babe who had been dancing in a night-club chorus till a few evenings before. From the play, the tycoon took her on a dizzy round of gay spots, and finally, delighted with her understanding ways, pressed a diamond clip into her hot little palm. "You darling man," she cooed, "it's such a business doing pleasure with you!"

A stranger from the East wandered into Slip Muldoon's Crazy Gulch Saloon and tried to cash a check for a hundred dollars. Slip leaned across the bar and assured the Easterner in a stage whisper, "You look like an all-right character and your check is probably good for a hundred thousand bucks. But I don't trust them big New York banks. They'll probably gyp both of us!"

At one of those unbearably fancy new candy stores on Fifth Avenue, seemingly modeled after the boudoir of a big-time French courtesan, the wife of the editor of a Jewish newspaper wandered in to sample the wares. "I'll take five pounds of those chocolates over there," she decided. "Modom means the bon bons, no doubt," a suave clerk in a cutaway corrected gently. "I also would like five pounds of those cookies," continued the lady. "Ah," breathed the clerk, "our petits fours. Shall we deliver your purchase in our Rolls limousine now drawn up before the portals?" "Nah," said the lady. "I'll carry it home myself." This was too much for the elegant clerk. "Don't be silly," he burst out. "Why schlepp a package that big around the streets?"

A prosperous-looking gent approached the manager of one of Miami Beach's swankiest new hostelries and asked to be shown the best available room. The manager led him to the most expensive suite in the establishment, pointing out, "This overlooks the ocean." The customer said it wouldn't do. The manager took him to his second-best accommodation, saying, "This isn't on the ocean, of course, but it does overlook our steam-heated swimming pool." Again the customer demurred. When he also rejected a third suite, "overlooking the tropical garden," the manager became a trifle impatient, and asked, "Just what have you got in mind, sir?" The customer announced firmly, "What I'm looking for is a room that overlooks the rent."

There have been so many new luxury hotels erected in Miami Beach in the past twelve months that the current fashion is to accost any tourist, ask him where he's stopping, and regardless of his reply, sneer, "That's last year's hotel."

A well-lubricated drummer staggered into a hotel lobby, and picked up a pen to register. As he did so a remarkable facsimile of a bedbug crawled across the desk. The drummer recoiled and informed the reception clerk, "I've been in lots of hotels, and I've been bitten by some mighty smart bedbugs, but—hic—this is the first time one ever came down to see what room I was getting!"

"Miss Potter," reproved her landlady, "I definitely thought I saw you sneaking a young gentleman up to your room with you last night." "You're not the only one," agreed Miss Potter. "I thought so too."

The Algonquin's famous boniface, the late Frank Case, loved William Faulkner personally, but was no admirer of his tortuous prose and grim pictures of depravity in the old South. Faulkner met him in the lobby one morning and complained, "I have kind of an upset stomach today." "Ah," sympathized Case, "something you wrote, no doubt?"

"Henry darling," said the blushing bride as the honeymooners drove up to the portico of the St. Regis, "let's try to convince all

the hangers-on in the lobby that we've been married for ages."
"Okay, my love," said Henry dubiously, "but do you think you
can carry four suitcases?"

Two Catskill hotel proprietors met on a train to New York. "Nu,
Sam," said one, "how's business this summer?" "I'll tell you,
Myron," was the reply, "we've got them sleeping under the beds.
The roof leaks."

Mrs. Goldschmidt is never going to let her husband talk her
into vacationing at sumptuous Morpheus Arms in the Catskills
again. "In the first place," she explains, "all the young girls did all
day was look for husbands. And in the second place, all the husbands did was look for young girls."

The late Ernie Byfield, boniface of Chicago's Ambassador East
Hotel, had his own way of expressing himself. A friend met him,
obviously elated, on the street of a Swiss village one day. "Why so
happy?" asked the friend. Byfield explained, "I just made a sucker
out of the Alps. I climbed them in spats."

The manager of a swanky hotel at French Lick stumbled over a
porter who was crouching in the corridor shining a pair of shoes.
"Ichabod," remonstrated the manager, "haven't I told you a hundred times not to clean shoes in the corridor, but to take them
down to the basement?" "Can't do it this time, boss," said Ichabod.
"The man in this room says he's from Scotland, and he's hanging
on to the laces."

One of the great stars of Hollywood cowboy sagas wired Toots Shor, the restaurateur, "Arriving New York in time for dinner, November ninth. Reserve table for two." Shor cautiously wired back, "Are you bringing your girl or your horse?"

A merchant in Allentown comes to New York twice a month to buy goods, and his favorite place to dine on such visits is a midtown restaurant that features not only good beef but four walls full of photographs of great movie stars, jockeys, and ball players, all autographed with messages of undying affection to the proprietor, Pasquale. After a while, the merchant couldn't help noticing that none of these glamour pusses was ever seen dining at the restaurant in person. Most of the patrons, in fact, invariably looked as though they, too, had just gotten off a train from Allentown. So he called over a waiter and grumbled, "Hey, how come I never see any of the big shots whose pictures you've got coming here in person. Have you ever spotted any of them yourself?" The waiter assured the merchant gravely, "Mister, I been working here myself for eight years, *and I never even met Pasquale!*"

Robert Haas knows a man who actually saw flying saucers. He walked up behind a plump waitress in a diner with an extended fishing pole in his hand.

August Belmont, famous epicure and member of New York and Newport's old "400," was once a guest of Robert Louis Stevenson in San Francisco. Stevenson took him to a certain restaurant off Market Street, and said, "An amazing feature of this place is that no waiter is ever permitted to say that any dish whatever is lacking from the menu. Ask for a slice of the moon and the waiter will solemnly march off to the kitchen to get it for you. Then he'll come back and tell you solemnly they're just out of it."

"I'll try them out," laughed Belmont, and ordered a double order of roast behemoth, rare. The waiter jotted down the order, only to report a moment later, "I'm very sorry . . ." "Oh ho," nodded Belmont. "You have no behemoth, eh?" "We have plenty of behemoth," said the waiter sharply, "but the truth is it's all so well done I know you wouldn't like it."

At last a rich man has been discovered who has a kind word to say about the U. S. Treasury Department! His name is Bill Goetz, a famous movie tycoon, art collector, and owner of the race horse "Your Host."

You may have read how Goetz bought a hitherto uncatalogued self-portrait of Van Gogh called "Study by Candlelight" for $45,-000 in Europe, and imported it to his home in California. Then a storm broke. Many connoisseurs said it was genuine. An equal

number declared it bogus. Goetz told me how he figured a way to make the U. S. Treasury render a final verdict. Here's his story:

According to statutes on the books, art masterpieces may be imported into our country free, but on reproductions there is an impost of 10 per cent of the purchase price.

Goetz shipped his controversial Van Gogh back to Amsterdam, then reimported it, valued at $50,000. The first time it came over, customs officers had accepted it as an original without question, but now the hubbub and excitement put them in a pretty quandary.

"Why not reduce the estimated value to $500?" the Treasury men begged Goetz. "Then you pay only a nominal $50 duty, and we're off the hook." "Nothing doing," said Goetz firmly. "If it's an original—and I'm convinced that it is—I don't pay a bloody cent. If it's a copy, I pay my $5,000 duty like a good citizen."

Result: The Treasury Department had to hire the greatest art experts in the land to decide the issue. They finally rendered their verdict—the picture is genuine! Back on the wall of the Goetz study it went, now worth conservatively five times its purchase price, and the dealers who once derided Goetz as a sucker have retreated disconsolately into their galleries muttering, "If you've got to Van Gogh, you've got to Van Gogh."

In England, a famous painter of our own day, the late Sir John Lavery, stared fixedly at a lady at a party, strode to her side and confessed, "I don't recall your name, but your features are certainly familiar to me."

"They jolly well ought to be," she told him sharply. "I paid you five thousand pounds to paint them!"

The late Lord Duveen, most spectacular art dealer of our time, operated on the theory that Europe had plenty of art while America had plenty of money—and that it was his job to provide better balance. He sold one client—Mr. Jules Bache—so many expensive paintings that when Miss Green, director of the Morgan Library, first saw the Bache collection she murmured "How utterly Duveen!" S. N. Behrman, who has written Duveen's story, says that he made millionaire clients seek *him* out; he never made the first approach. Informed, for instance, that Mr. Edsel Ford had begun to acquire an expensive art collection, Duveen observed loftily, "He's not ready for me yet. Let him go on buying. Some day he'll be big enough for me!" Some of Duveen's clients —Mellon, Rockefeller, Frick, Morgan, Kress—thought nothing of paying him half a million dollars for an art masterpiece. They agreed with his oft-proclaimed theory that "You can get all the pictures you want at ten thousand dollars apiece—but to find ones worth half a million—I say, that takes doing!"

Children could resist Lord Duveen's powers of persuasion no more successfully than well-heeled adult collectors. One day at the seaside, Duveen's young daughter refused to dive into the briny; it was much too cold, she declared. Lord Duveen gravely gathered some sticks on the beach, started a bonfire, borrowed a kettle, boiled some water in it, and then poured it into the Atlantic Ocean. Completely satisfied, his daughter dove in without the slightest hesitation.

At a certain stage of life there comes to every person the irrepressible urge to collect something. Paintings, books, china, rare coins and stamps provide the usual outlet for such yearnings, but some notable individualists have gone much further afield.

The late Crosby Gaige, for instance, had a passion for models of useless inventions, such as mechanical back-scratchers. Most of them looked like the handiwork of Rube Goldberg, and they took up a whole floor of an office building by the time he died. A man in Springfield, Massachusetts, has one of the oddest collections of all. He goes in for dinosaur tracks! He sent one of his treasures, imprinted in a block of solid stone, to his son for Christmas last year. The son was not too appreciative—especially when the stone fell on his toe and laid him up for five weeks.

There are a number of allegedly living and solvent citizens (Jim Marshall does the alleging) whose names and addresses make complete sentences. Here's the evidence:

Hans R. Dirty, Jr., Goan, Wash.
Quoth D. Raven, Never, Mo.
G. Thirza Mighty, Pritty, Miss.
Ide Lamy, Down, N.D.
Lettice Finder, Shady, Del.
F. U. Pager, Income, Tex.
I. M. Phelan, Slightly, Ill.
Daniel Inner, Lyons, Tenn.
Wish I. Newther, Reese, N.Y.
C. U. Sunday, Early, Mass.
Allis Frenza, Deadan, Conn.
R. R. Crossing, Look, N.C.
Will U. Raider, Cookie, Ga.

R is for
RAILROADS

A seedy-looking gent stumbled into a parlor-car seat directly opposite a very correct Boston lady, who held on her lap an equally haughty, bespectacled little girl. The lady quite obviously found the proximity of the seedy gent objectionable. In fact, she took the extraordinary step of leaning across the aisle and whispering, "I think you should know that my little girl is just recuperating from a bad case of smallpox, which is still probably contagious." "Don't let that worry you for a moment," said the seedy one, unperturbed. "I'm going to cut my throat in the first tunnel anyhow."

There's a station on a one-track Maine branch line to which passengers descend via a rickety staircase. Alongside it is a chute used to slide down packing cases and heavy baggage.

Local tradition has it that an elderly lady once came whizzing down the chute, clutching her hat in one hand and a straw valise in the other. At the bottom she pulled herself together and exclaimed, "You'd think a big railroad company would make it a little easier for passengers to get down to their ding-busted trains!"

146

Two lads were sauntering along a railroad track when one suddenly stopped, picked up a girl's arm, and exclaimed, "I believe that's Gwendolyn!" "Don't be silly," chided the other. "How can you jump to the conclusion that's any particular girl just by seeing an arm?" A moment later, the first lad discovered a leg along the right of way and repeated, "I'm surer than ever that's Gwendolyn." "Nonsense," scoffed his friend. "It's not Gwendolyn at all." The same argument ensued when another arm, and then a torso turned up, but then the second lad spied a girl's head next to the track. Examining the head intently, he cried, "By George, it *is* Gwendolyn!" Then he entreated, "Gwendolyn! For Pete's sake! *Pull yourself together!*"

A little man in a Pennsylvania Railroad day-coach created quite a stir recently with his loud and repeated claims that he really was General George Washington traveling incognito. Of course, nobody believed him—till he got off at Mt. Vernon.

The president of a great Southern railroad is noted for his patience and humility. He says he got a lesson he never forgot the first day he was appointed station master in a tiny Mississippi way-stop. Two Negro farmers came along to ask some questions regarding a bill of lading, and the new official decided to put on the dog. The Negroes waited patiently while he bustled about the station doing nothing, and then one said very distinctly to the other, "Dat's life for you, brother! De littler de station, de bigger de agent." What the young official learned that moment helped make him president of the road!

When the Mobile and Southern Railroad explained to Deacon Smedley that a proposed cut-off would run right through the spot where his barn stood, and offered him ten times the worth of the property for his consent, Smedley astounded everybody, his wife in particular, by turning a deaf ear to the proposal. He defended his stand to his outraged wife by shouting, "Dang it, do ye think I'm goin' to keep running out to that barn day and night to open and shut the door every time they want to run a train through?"

A band of hoboes enjoyed an unexpected windfall when they discovered a trim forty-foot yacht tied down to a flatcar in a freight yard at Barstow, California, not long ago.

The yacht was being shipped across the country by Charles and Jessie Hilton. The hoboes moved in and lived the carefree life of the bounding main until they were discovered in Kansas. They scattered hastily, crying, "All ashore" and "Cast anchor," and lost their sea legs in the historic port of Wichita.

It seems to me that an ingenious script writer could build a hilarious motion picture around this episode. The Hiltons, meanwhile, are building a new yacht.

When the conductor on an Arkansas local came through collecting tickets, an old gentleman simply couldn't find his in any pocket. Suddenly a man across the aisle laughed and said, "Jeb, you're holding it in your teeth." The conductor punched the ticket and passed on down the aisle. "Jeb, you're sure getting absent-minded," pursued the man across the aisle. "Absent-minded nothing," whispered old Jeb angrily. "I was chewing off last year's date."

Harpo Marx came down to the Pasadena station one day to see a friend off for the East. He was engaging in some characteristic clowning on the platform when he noticed two Helen Hokinson ladies gazing with undisguised horror from the diner on the train the friend was boarding. Impulsively, Harpo hopped aboard, rushed up to the ladies' table in the diner, sprinkled salt on their menu and gulped it down.

With no change of expression, one of them summoned the steward and commanded, "Kindly give us another menu. Somebody has eaten ours."

Winston Churchill, like all men who do a dozen things at the same time, is always pressed to keep appointments and arrive at stations, piers, and airports on time. Asked why he missed so many trains and boats, Mr. Churchill explained, "I'm a sporting man, my boy. I always give them a fair chance to get away."

A returned traveler from Wales reports that whenever the through trains stop at Llanfechpwllgogerych the guards simply call out, "If anybody's getting out here, this is it."

Most people, at one time or another, have fallen asleep in a railroad car, and awakened somewhere in the yards. An unfortunate in South Africa went them one better recently, however. He curled up for a nap in an empty day coach. During the night the coach was moved to the repairs depot. When dawn broke, the sleeper yawned luxuriously, took one glance out of the window, and let out a yelp of horror. His car, suspended from a big crane, was dangling two hundred feet above the track.

Eli Bohnen, of Providence, remembers a Baptist minister in a New Mexico town who rushed down to the station every single day to watch the Sunset Limited go by. There was no chore he wouldn't interrupt to carry out this ritual. Members of his congregation deemed his eccentricity juvenile and frivolous, and asked him to give it up. "No, gentlemen," he said firmly. "I preach your sermons, teach your Sunday school, bury your dead, marry you, run your charities, chairman every drive it pleases you to conduct. I won't give up seeing that Southern Pacific train every day. I love it. It's the only thing that passes through this town that I don't have to push!"

Averell Harriman, who once ran the whole Union Pacific Railroad, was present when a young minister gave his first sermon in a Sun Valley church. It went on and on, and several members of the congregation predicted he'd never do. Harriman was more optimistic, however. "I considered it a good trial run," he said. "The young man's service will improve as soon as he gets better terminal facilities."

It was in Utah that the last spike was driven in America's first railroad to the Pacific—at Promontory on May 10, 1869—but history books have spared us some of the less glamorous details. In the first place, the Union Pacific Special from the East was held up by floods and arrived three days late. Chinese laborers on the Central Pacific and the Irishmen who had laid the tracks for the U.P. amused themselves in the interim by taking pot shots at one another. There were some forty casualties, including one innocent bystander from San Francisco. In the second place, the ceremonies dragged on too long; the crowd shivered in an icy wind, and drifted away before the climax. In the third place, Governor Leland Stanford of California, chosen to drive in the last golden spike (it was removed immediately), lifted his head on the backswing, missed the spike entirely, and fell on his face in the mud. An alert telegrapher, however, simulated the blow with his key, and a waiting multitude on both coasts (including Wall Street) cheered the completion of the first transcontinental railroad span. Luckily for Governor Stanford, television was still eighty years away.

R is for RELIGION

Fulton J. Sheen relates that shortly after his elevation to the rank of Bishop he made the first of his many appearances on television, and stopped for a cup of coffee at the drugstore in the building where the studio was located, with his red cape already in place. The girl at the counter, obviously used to serving actors in every kind of costume, took the red cape very much in stride and asked blithely, "What's yours, Cock Robin?"

Joe Harrington, the Boston sage, tells of a Sunday-school teacher who suddenly stopped reading a passage in the Bible and asked her pupils, "Why do you believe in God?" She got a variety of answers, some full of simple faith, others obviously insincere. The one that stopped her cold came from the son of one of Boston's best-known ministers. He frowned, and answered thoughtfully, "I guess it just runs in our family."

In the Breton village of Cancale, Roger Vercel watched the traditional ceremony of the regional bishop blessing the fishermen before they set out for their annual two-month expedition on the high seas in their tiny vessels. Vercel said to the bishop, "They all revere you deeply, yet they all vote Communist. Can't you do anything about that?" "It's difficult," sighed the bishop. "They know that God controls the storms and tides, but the Communists, alas, control the price of fish."

Sister Carmelita won the big final game at a church bingo party and decided to indulge a craving she had concealed for years. She bought herself a beautiful fur coat. The day it arrived, she donned it hastily and walked proudly down Main Street, admired by all and sundry. Suddenly, however, her bishop drew alongside in his shiny new limousine and chided her for not putting her windfall to better use. "May I remind you, Sister Carmelita," he concluded,

"that no saint ever has been known to require an expensive fur coat?" "Quite true," agreed Sister Carmelita cheerfully, "but I'd also like to know of one character in the Bible who rolled around the Holy Land in an eight-cylinder limousine."

Three lads fell to boasting about the earning capacities of their respective fathers. Said the doctor's son, "My pa operated on a movie producer last month and sent him a bill for a cool five thousand." The lawyer's son spoke up, "Shucks, what's that? My old man was the mouthpiece for a big racketeer a week ago and got a fee of ten grand for one day's work—all paid in crisp new thousand-dollar bills." The minister's son said quietly, "On Sunday, my father preached a sermon in church, and it took eight men to bring in the money."

An old bishop in the nation's capital was sick to death of the socials and embassy parties he was expected to attend every other afternoon. At one of them he entered wearily, glanced sourly at the over-familiar cast of characters, and sank into the nearest chair. The hostess asked coyly, "A spot of tea, Bishop?" "No tea," he growled. "Coffee, Bishop?" "No coffee." An understanding woman, she whispered in his ear, "Scotch and water, Bishop?" Said the bishop, brightening, "No water."

A group of world leaders in the Presbyterian Church met in Scotland for a conference and, on a warm summer's afternoon, went off to explore the beautiful countryside. Coming to a temporary bridge that spanned a swift-running stream, they started confidently to cross it. When they were half way over, the bridge keeper suddenly appeared and hollered that the bridge had been declared unsafe. The spokesman for the church party didn't quite hear the keeper's admonition and called back, "It's all right, my friend. We're Presbyterians from the conference." The bridge keeper replied, "If ye dinna get off the bridge this minute ye'll all be Baptists!"

The first time four-year-old Mary was taken to church by her parents, she was absolutely fascinated by the earnest young minister, high in his pulpit, who was given to involved rhetoric and wild waving of his arms. Finally Mary whispered to her mother, "What will we do if he ever gets out?"

A distinguished Broadway star is known far and wide for the deep religious strain in her character. A few seasons ago, just before the opening of an important play, she announced to the cast, "I don't pay no mind to what any of you think. I'm going to pray for our success tonight." Thereupon she dropped to her knees on the center of the stage, cast her eyes heavenward, and implored, "Oh, Lord, help all of us give a fine performance this evening. Let me give the best that's in me. Let the rest of the company make the hits of their lives. Let the critics approve. And one thing more, oh, Lord, keep that blank-blank stage director from lousing up this play for us."

A minister in Oklahoma was preaching such a powerful sermon that an excited (and beautiful) young lady in the balcony leaned over too far and crashed through the railing. Her dress caught in a chandelier, and she was suspended in mid-air. The minister noted her undignified position and thundered to his congregation, "Any person who looks up at poor Miss Duggan will be stricken blind." A deacon in the third row whispered to his companion, "I'm going to risk one eye."

There's a venerable psychotic patient on Welfare Island who spends her entire time reading the Bible. She explains, "I'm cramming for the finals."

The parson's wife in a small Connecticut town is a wonder at making a little go a long way, and boasts that she never throws away one scrap of edible food. One of her dinners consisted entirely of leftovers. The parson viewed the food on the table with some distaste and began picking at his food in silence. "My dear," reproved his wife, "you've forgotten to ask the blessing." "If you can point out one item on the menu," he answered sharply, "that hasn't been blessed at least three times before, I'll see what a little praying can do for it."

The new minister looked at Squire Canfield coldly and said, "I'm told you went to the ball game instead of church Sunday." "That's a lie," cried Squire Canfield hotly, "and I've got the fish to prove it."

A young clergyman, about to preach his first sermon, was a bundle of nerves as he waited in the vestry. Would his voice carry? Would he hold his fashionable audience? Above all, did he look his best? "Dear me," he reflected aloud, "if only there was a glass here." A moment later the verger tapped him on the shoulder and whispered, "Here's a whole bottle. All I had to do was mention your name."

When Parson Johnson saw Mrs. Sumter, whom he roundly detested, coming up his garden path, he sought refuge upstairs in the study and remained hidden for a full hour. Finally he risked calling down to his wife, "Has that horrible bore gone yet?" His wife, equal to any occasion, answered sweetly, "Yes, dear, she went long ago. Mrs. Sumter is here now."

A young man barged into a minister's study, a lovely young lady in tow, and exclaimed, "We want to get married. I beg you to make the ceremony as brief as possible. Here are our credentials. I assure you they're in order. Those ladies knitting in the corner will do fine as witnesses." The minister, amused, performed the ritual, gratefully pocketed a fifty-dollar bill, then protested, "Remember the old adage about marrying in haste, my children. What's your hurry?" The young man, already half way to the door, explained over his shoulder, "We're double parked!"

R is for
ROMANCE

A bashful swain wrote to an advice-to-the-lovelorn column in San Francisco, "Last night I treated a young lady to dinner, theatre, a night club, and a twenty-mile ride home in a taxi. Do you think I should have kissed her good night?" "Certainly not," answered the sarcastic editor. "You did enough for her as it is!"

Hoarsely the impassioned swain begged, "Whisper those three little words that will make me walk on air." So the debutante sweetly told him, "Go hang yourself."

Rupert Hughes claims he knows the origin of kissing. "A prehistoric man," avers Hughes, "discovered one day that salt helped him survive the fierce summer heat. He also discovered he could get the salt by licking a companion's cheek. The next thing he observed was that the process became ever so much more interesting when the companion belonged to the opposite sex. First thing you know, the whole tribe had forgotten all about salt."

There was a long line waiting to use the only public telephone booth in the neighborhood, and when a young thing with blonde curls and a huge vanity bag strapped over her shoulder prepared to enter, the experienced men behind her sighed in unison and resigned themselves to the inevitable. The young thing, however, sensed what was going on in their minds. "Don't you all fret," she told them sweetly. "I'll only be a minute. I just want to hang up on him!"

Somebody has defined adolescence as the period when a girl begins to powder and a boy begins to puff. Another says a boy has reached that stage when he knows why a strapless gown must be held up, but doesn't understand how.

Roger Price is fond of extolling the virtues of his nineteen-year-old cousin Sally, who certainly sounds like an unusual lass. For instance, cites Roger, she went to one party where she had the boys neglecting every other girl in the place because she was the only one who had the sense to come naked. Another time she was approached by a virile stranger who slipped a note into her hot little palm that read, "You are the only woman I ever have loved. Come to my room, 648, at the Grand Hotel at midnight." Sally wasn't sure he was sincere, however, because the note was mimeographed.

Humphrey Jones, known as the great lover in the wholesale house where he worked, seemed so listless and depressed one morning that Coombs, at the next desk, called over, "Hey, Humphrey, I'll bet that new girl you've been raving about gave you the heave-ho." "It isn't that," said Jones glumly, "but I'm afraid she isn't quite so exclusive as she had led me to believe.

She moved into a new apartment last Tuesday, and you know what she spent all Wednesday doing? Going from one phone booth to another, changing her number on the walls!"

A winsome chick gave up her job at the Copacabana night club to marry an auto executive in Detroit. "He's the knight I always dreamed would appear out of the West to win me," she gurgled. "He's tall, dark, and has some."

Bernard Shaw's criticism of the marriage ritual: "When two people are under the influence of the most violent, most insane, most delusive and most transient of passions, they are required to solemnly swear they will remain in that excited, abnormal and exhausting condition continuously until death do them part."

"Yes, sir," said the installment furniture salesman to a prospective bridegroom, "you just furnish the bride and we'll do the rest." "If you don't mind," suggested the bridegroom, "let's change places!"

"Alone at last," sighed a bridegroom to his bride—but he was wrong, for at that precise moment, a pistol was poked into his ribs, and a gruff voice commanded, "Put 'em up." The intruder, obviously experienced, headed straight for the jewel box on the dresser, but then he got a real glimpse of the bride in her negligee. Hastily drawing a circle on the floor with his heel, he commanded the groom, "Into this circle, lug, and if you move out of it, I'll shoot you full of holes." So the poor groom stood in the circle and watched in misery while the intruder made love to his

bride. When he finally made his exit—having quite forgotten the
jewels, incidentally—the bride turned on the groom and cried,
"How could you stand there and watch a total stranger making
love to your wife? Are you a man or a mouse?"

"A man," proclaimed the bridegroom vehemently. "You didn't
notice, I expect, but every time that fellow had his back turned, I
stuck my foot right out of the circle."

The statistical department of Brides House, Inc., bullish by
nature on everything pertaining to matrimony, announces that
the average wedding presents a whopping $4820 sales opportu-
nity to alert merchants. Furthermore, that figure includes only
what's bought by the bride, groom, and members of the wedding
troupe, and does not take into account the gifts. The chief items
of expenditure are: household equipment, $1633; home furnish-
ings, $1820; dresses, $360; coats and suits, $225; lingerie, $219;
luggage, $180; shoes, $106; linens and bedding, $181; millinery,
$96. Paste these figures in your hat, and the next time somebody
groans "What price matrimony?" you'll have a pat answer ready!
Brides House also predicts that 13 persons out of every 1000 in

the country will choose a mate during the coming year—and Dale Carnegie will see to it that most of them read "Ideal Marriage" before taking the vows.

Dr. Morris Fishbein, one of the medical marvels of the age that does not come in the form of pills, writes that he attended a wedding recently where he found the one male dressed in tuxedo standing mournfully in an alcove. "I take it," hazarded the good doctor, "that you are the groom." "You take it wrong," the mournful one replied. "I was eliminated in the semi-finals."

An item for the "father of the bride" department from Hasbrouck Heights, New Jersey: A delicate young bride-to-be sighed to her mother, "Oh dear, there are so many things to do before the wedding, and I don't want to overlook the most insignificant detail." "Don't you worry your pretty little head," said the mother grimly. "I'll see that he's there."

A rueful bridegroom told an inquiring reporter, "I never knew what happiness was until I got married—and then it was too late."

On the porch of Vanderschlitz Manor Mrs. Nussbaum mourned, "My boy never should have married that Davis girl. In a year she turned him into a pauper." "Really?" nodded Mrs. Gross pleasantly. "A girl or a boy?"

S is for SPORTS

Thanks to the coaxial cable, about forty million television fans can now see every play in baseball's annual classic, the World Series, with their own eyes. 'Twas not ever thus. In the old days, the nearest a real fan could get to a Series game was a seat behind a post in right field. The good seats were reserved for politicians, movie stars and Broadway big shots who might not know a squeeze play from an umpire, but thought this was the place to be when the newsreel cameras started grinding.

Miss Lily Pons, the beautiful coloratura soprano, was thus discovered in a box seat for the opening game of a recent Series. "I didn't know you were a baseball fan," commented a reporter.

"Indeed I am," enthused Miss Pons. "I wouldn't miss this game for the world. By the way, who is playing?"

Jerome Herman Dean, better known as "Dizzy" to admiring baseball fans all over the country, is even better behind the mike than he was on the mound pitching for the old St. Louis Cardinal gas-house gang in the thirties—and higher praise than that hath no diamond enthusiast.

Ted Shane has dug up a Dizzy Dean anecdote I never heard before. Seems the Diz once bet a crony two bits he could fan Joe

163

Di Maggio's big brother, Vince, every time he faced him one afternoon. Vince obligingly whiffed his first three times up, but on his fourth trip to the plate, lifted a harmless little pop back of the plate. Dean hollered to his catcher, "Drop it, or I'm ruint!" Then he burned over the next pitch for strike three.

Dizzy Dean thinks he knows how Red Russia could be brought into line. "I'd get me a buncha bats and balls and learn them kids behind the Iron Curtain how to play baseball instead of totin' rifles and swallerin' lies. And if Joe Stallion ever learnt how much dough there was in the concessions at a ball park, he'd quit commanism and get into a honest business."

One batter, according to Arthur Daly, who never had the slightest difficulty solving the delivery of the great Dizzy Dean was Bill Terry, the famous Giant first-baseman. One afternoon Terry almost tore Dean's legs off with a wicked liner through the box. The next time up he scorched Diz's ear with a sizzler that went rocketing into center field. His third hit almost tore off Dean's glove.

Pepper Martin sauntered over from third base and suggested to the outraged Dean, "Dizzy, I don't think you're playing this bird Terry deep enough!"

Jimmy Dykes, the famous baseball player and manager, tells this story on himself.

When he first joined the A's back in 1918, he struck out four times in his first game. On his next turn Connie Mack used a pinch hitter. Jimmy sulked on the bench, but the understanding Connie soothed him. "I suppose you know why I took you out," said Mack. "You see, the American League record for striking out is five times in one game, and I didn't want you to tie it in your very first big league game."

Joe McCarthy recalls a year in the Depression when the mighty
Babe Ruth was asked to submit to the first salary cut of his career.
To say that he demurred is putting it mildly. He insisted on his
customary eighty-thousand-dollar contract. "But, Babe," protested
an official of the Yankee ball club, "these are trying times. That's
more money than Hoover got last year for being President of the
United States." "I know," persisted the Babe, "but I had a better
year than Hoover."

Add this story to the saga of the wacky Brooklyn Dodger baseball squad that toiled without signals (because they couldn't remember any) under the indulgent management of the late Wil-
bert Robinson. "Uncle Robbie's" particular problem child was
Babe Herman, who could whack that old apple a mile, but never
learned big-league fielding or base-running finesse. Herman could
always melt Uncle Robbie's wrath with a wisecrack. His little
son also had a special spot in the rotund manager's heart. One
day, however, when the kid climbed trustingly onto Robbie's lap,
he was dumped unceremoniously to the Ebbets Field turf. The
manager pointed an accusing finger at the six-year-old and
barked, "Why ain't your old man hitting?"

The same Babe Herman was informed by a downtown Brooklyn bank one day that an impostor was signing his name to worthless checks and cashing them several times a week. "The next time
he comes in," proposed Babe, "take him out in the back yard and
knock a few flies his way. If he catches any, you'll know it isn't
me."

The venerable Negro pitching star, Satchel Paige, is used mainly in relief roles these days, and accordingly gets mighty few chances to show his batting prowess. He did come to the plate in a late inning of a tie game at the St. Louis park one evening, however, and rapped a hot grounder between shortstop and third that almost any other player in the league could have beaten out with ease. "Satch" was thrown out by four steps. "Why didn't you run?" cried the Brownie manager. "Counter," said Satch. "Whaddya mean, 'counter'?" roared the manager. Satch explained, "Counter mah feet hurt."

The New York Yankees are generally regarded as aristocrats in the major-league baseball hierarchy, but their star catcher, Yogi Berra, travels around the country with a valise that looks as though it saw service in the Mexican War in the 1840s. A baseball newshawk asked Yogi, "Why don't you treat yourself to a new suitcase?" "What for?" argued Yogi. "The only time I ever use it is when I travel." Earl Wilson pointed out Yogi to a visiting Hollywood glamour girl at Nicky Blair's restaurant one evening. "That's the best catcher in the American League," said Earl. "Zat so?" gurgled the starlet. "What did he catch?"

Svenborg managed to stay on the Yale football squad all season, although he never got into a game. His only contribution consisted in acting as a tackling dummy at practice sessions, and sitting huddled up in a robe at the end of the bench during games. The Harvard fray, however, produced so many minor injuries that, near the end of the final quarter, Coach Hickman had poured every member of the squad but Svenborg into the line-up. Time was called while still another Yale stalwart was carried off the field. The coach's eyes traveled along the empty bench until they encountered Svenborg. A wild hope surged through Svenborg's veins. "Gee, coach," he marveled. "Are you gonna send me in?" "I should say not," snapped Hickman. "Just get up. I'm gonna send in the bench!"

Remember a football team that came up from the South years ago from tiny Centre College and beat the then-mighty Harvard eleven? The nickname for the valiant little Centre squad was "the praying colonels" because at crucial junctures of a contest all the boys would kneel and pray. H. Allen Smith avers that one day in the dressing room, the Centre coach suddenly cried, "Down to your knees, boys, here comes Grantland Rice!"

Kip Taylor, Oregon State mentor, has the final solution for the regulation of big-time football: one squad for offense, one for defense—and one to attend classes.

In these days when college football stadiums seat 90,000 or more spectators, it is interesting to note the comment made once by Andrew W. White, co-founder of Cornell University and its first president. Asked for permission to send the Cornell squad to Ann Arbor for a game, he replied indignantly, "I will not permit thirty men to travel four hundred miles to agitate a bag of wind."

"Pop" Gabardine, coach of a Midwestern football team, had seen his charges trampled eight Saturday afternoons in a row, the last time by a humiliating score of 55 to 0. When the squad regathered the following Monday, "Pop" said bitterly, "For the last game of the season, we might as well forget all the trick plays I tried to teach you dimwits. We're going back to fundamentals. Let's go! Lesson number one: this object I am holding is known as a football. Lesson number . . ." At this point, Coach Gabardine was interrupted by a worried fullback in the front row, who pleaded, "Hey, Pop, not so fast!"

California's Governor Earl Warren had to submit to quite a ribbing from Governor Adlai Stevenson of Illinois over the repeated failure of California's entries in the Rose Bowl football game to cope with elevens from the Midwest's "Big Ten." "Boast on," said Governor Warren finally, and with resignation, "but remember this: a whale never gets really harpooned until he comes up to spout."

Between halves of a tough professional football game, three stars of the winning team fell to talking about the circumstances that surrounded their leaving college to play for money. "I was a senior at Cornell," said the first, "and got grounded on calculus. I couldn't even begin to know what the prof was talking about." "It was advanced trigonometry that did me in," said the second. "In fact, it ran me right out of Kansas State in my junior year." The third player, late of U.C.L.A., sat staring moodily into space. Suddenly he spoke. "Say, did you boys ever run into a subject called long division?"

When Alfred Vanderbilt was elected President of the Thoroughbred Racing Association, he made a tour of all the leading tracks in the country to inspect the plants and racing conditions. Arriving in Lexington, Kentucky, he found a big sign strung across Main Street that read, "Welcome Vanderbilt." "Boy," he said appreciatively, "they sure take their horse racing seriously in this town." "Shucks, Al," his host informed him, "that sign isn't for you. Kentucky's football team is playing Vanderbilt University here tomorrow."

Millie Considine came back from the Kentucky Derby with a
tale about an old Louisville hostelry that traditionally named one
of its rooms for the winner of the big annual racing classic. There
was a Zev room, a Gallant Fox room, a Whirlaway room, etc.
After the 1946 Derby, however, the management was reluctantly
compelled to abandon the idea. Winner that year was Assault.

Jonathan Daniels probably covered a thousand horse races—
Kentucky Derbies and other classics of the track—during his
newspaper career, but none of them made the impression on him
occasioned by a race between five camels at a Carolina carnival
early in the century. Nobody remembers who persuaded the
owners of the five camels to stage the race, but the first thing anybody knew, news of the contest spread throughout the state, and
people began to bet on the outcome. Perplexed bookies established initial odds of four to one against all five camels, but just
before the race so many big bets were planked down on the one
named Ben Ali—all of them, apparently, made by the Arab owners
—that the bookies grew suspicious, and refused all further bets.
Furthermore, they watched the race with eagle eyes for any sign
of dirty work.

The race, to all intents and purposes, however, was fairly run.
All five Arab owners pressed their mounts with equal fervor and
determination, and when Ben Ali won easily, the bookies could
find no excuse for withholding payment to the winners. One of
them, his exchequer badly depleted, asked the Arab who had
finished third, "What made all you birds bet everything on Ben
Ali?"

The Arab explained, with a grin, "Mister, Ben Ali is what is
known in our country as a bell camel. From the day of their birth,
camels are taught to follow the bell camel!"

A huntsman in Texas had a harrowing experience one night this fall. He had killed a huge rattlesnake outside his tent before supper, and, just before going off to sleep, decided that the rattles would make a nice memento. With a practiced hand, he cut off the rattles in the dark.

The sight that greeted him the next morning stood his hair on end. The snake he had killed still had its rattles!

An intrepid bear stalker was recounting his triumphs to the boys around the cracker barrel one midwinter night. "I guess my closest shave," he recalled, "came the day I was walking unsuspectingly along a narrow mountain path when suddenly a giant grizzly crept up behind me, locked my arms in a tight embrace and then began squeezing the life out of me."

"What did you do?" obliged one of the boys with the expected show of suspense. "What the dickens could I do?" groaned the huntsman. "I had to marry his daughter."

A prominent decoration in the Gumbiner living room was a moosehead—but it was hung upside down. Mrs. Gumbiner's explanation was, "Papa shot it while it was lying on its back."

My uncle Al likes fishing in Wisconsin, and is still boasting about the prize muskegon he caught back in 1893 or 1894. "I'll tell you how big that fish was," he's fond of saying on little or no provocation. "The guide took a picture of it for me, and the picture alone weighed sixteen pounds!"

Amateur horseshoe pitchers, content to make one ringer out of ten and hopeful only of landing all their shots within a foot of the stake, wavered between incredulity and despair when they read that Ted Allen, of Boulder, Colorado, established a world's record with twenty-nine consecutive *double* ringers! Allen also killed a rabbit at forty feet by hanging a horseshoe around its neck. Hank Bradshaw testifies that any tournament topnotcher can light a match tied to the stake with one shoe and extinguish it with the next. He also says most of them will give you ten to one you can rest your chin on the top of the stake while they throw ringers under it. That's *your* chin, brother: not mine!

Reminds me of the time Squire Parsons visited the State Fair and planked down $1.40 in "slim dimes—the tenth part of a dollar" to see fourteen consecutive performances of Señor Hidalgo hurling knives into a board and making a silhouette with them around the body of his buxom blonde wife. Finally the squire shuffled off for home muttering disgustedly, "Shucks, the durn fool just misses her every time."

A polo expert (rated at nine goals by the international committee) explained the difference between polo and other sports to writer Bob Sylvester. "With athletes in other games," he noted, "the first thing that usually gives out is the legs. In polo, it's the money."

"A golf game involves all kinds of problems," Nussbaum told his wife. "Take the match I had with that Scotch fellow McGregor at the civic center course this morning. We're all square at the seventeenth hole, playing a two-dollar nassau, when McGregor loses his ball in a thick rough. Naturally I go over and help him look for it, on account I don't want any monkey business from McGregor. He can't find his ball, however, and I start walking toward the green. Suddenly he yells after me, 'It's okay, Joe, here was that little ball of mine all the time.' I look back and there I see a ball right on the fairway, all beautifully teed up for a shot to the green, with McGregor happily pulling an approaching iron from his bag. And here, my dear, I am faced with a very serious problem. Just how am I going to be able to break the news to McGregor that all the time I've got his 'lost ball' in my pocket?"

The most believable golf story of the year appeared on the sports page of a Daytona Beach newspaper recently. It read, "At this point the gallery deserted the defending champion to watch Miss Blank, whose shorts were dropping on the green with astonishing regularity."

On the golf course at Echo Lake, Novelist Bud Kelland landed in a deep trap, and his three companions chuckled happily as they heard him blasting away out of sight. Back on the fairway, one asked, "How many shots did you have in that trap?" "Four," answered Bud. "We distinctly heard eight," he was told. "Remember where we are," he grumbled. "Four of them were echoes."

In the amusing *73 Years in a Sand Trap,* Fred Beck and O. K. Barnes tell of two confirmed rivals at the Lehigh Country Club in Allentown, Pa., who fought so consistently they finally agreed not to talk at all during a match.

All went smoothly and silently until the sixteenth hole, when the player identified as Doc walked ahead to a ball on the edge of the green while his opponent, Jack, climbed into a sand trap to play out. Jack took one swing, then another, and another, finally topping a shot clear across the green and into a trap on the other side. Then he whanged the ball back into trap number one.

As he wearily recrossed the green, Doc broke the long silence. "May I say one word?" he asked. "Well," snarled Jack, "what is it?" Doc replied, "You're playing with my ball."

T is for
TELEVISION
And Radio

Nine times out of ten, when you think your favorite television actor is wearing a white shirt, it's actually light blue or some other neutral color. The color white reflects a glare from the powerful overhead lights and casts an unflattering shadow over the actor's neckline.

With that thought in mind, Paul Hartman, who usually performs his burlesque dance routines in white tie and tails, ordered two stiff-bosomed evening shirts in blue. The mystified shirtmaker followed instructions—at $25 per instruction.

Hartman used the shirts with conspicuous success, and then consigned them to the laundry. But they didn't come back with either that week's wash or the next. They finally were delivered, accompanied by a note from the unhappy laundryman.

"We scrubbed and scrubbed these shirts," it read, "and finally succeeded in getting most of the blue out of them. If they are not absolutely white, please don't blame us."

◆

In a round-up of the year's funniest radio "fluffs," Joe Bryan awards palm leaves with clusters to:

Jerry Lawrence for "When the King and Queen arrive you will hear a twenty-one sun galoot."

174

A commentator from Korea for "This brings back memories of the Bulgian Belch."

Mel Allen for "It's smope-piking time."

Ken Allyn for "Visit your nearest A and Poo Feed Store."

André Baruch for "Good evening, ladies and gentlemen of the audio radiance."

Fred Utal (first prize!) for "Have you tried Buppert's Reer?"

Jack Benny's debut in the theatre, according to a man named Fred Allen, who claims to be an authority, was so far back in the woods that the manager was a bear. Furthermore, says Fred, Benny's salary for the week was paid in honey. Shortly thereafter Jack took up golf, continues Mr. Allen, but by the time he could afford to lose a ball, he couldn't hit it that far. Even Fred concedes, however, that Jack has *some* virtues. (The whole feud, of course, is strictly for laughs; the two are devoted friends.) "There's a little good in everybody, in fact," he concludes. "Even a Mickey Finn has a couple of drops of good whiskey in it."

In *No People Like Show People*, Maurice Zolotow adds another item to the Jack Benny saga. Jack was once so down on his luck that when his agent heard a New Jersey pop vaudeville palladium was offering twenty-five dollars for a novelty animal act, he cried, "I'll take it." He borrowed two mangy Pekingese pups from a friend, carried them on-stage in the Jersey theatre, tied them to a piece of scenery, and proceeded to wow the audience with funny stories and wheezings on his fiddle. The manager forked over the twenty-five dollars with the reservation that this certainly was the most peculiar animal act he ever did see. "Don't those pups do any tricks at all?" he demanded. "They sure do," said Jack airily, "but not at these prices."

At the entrance of the CBS studio, Jack Benny was stopped by a moocher who claimed to be an old vaudeville pal and put the bee on Jack for a two-dollar loan. "I'll pay you back if it's the last thing I do," promised the poor fellow as he pocketed the two greenbacks. Benny forgot all about the incident until about eight months later, when, to his surprise, he received a letter from the man, postmarked Denver. "I've struck it rich in Colorado, Jack," he boasted. "Everything broke right at the same time. Happy days are here again. I've got a great job and a society girl is going to marry me. Thanks for everything." The letter had a postscript. "I am enclosing one dollar on account of my debt. I'll send the other just as soon as I can spare it!"

Goodman Ace says he's discovered how really to enjoy television. "We do it all with a six-foot screen," he explains gravely, and when his visitor invariably expresses astonishment, he adds, "Yes, it's a Japanese screen, and we place it directly in front of the television set."

The happiest man he's met in years, insists Robert Q. Lewis, is the parking-lot attendant across the way from the CBS studio. After ten years of juggling expensive convertibles and coupés, he's finally passed his driving test.

Tallulah Bankhead's triumph as a radio M.C. inspired one jealous rival to remark, "Tallu's gotten so high-hat she pronounces the second 'l' in 'Lincoln.'" Groucho Marx calls her technique "the timing of the shrew." She once barked at Bob Hope, "Get off this stage until I call for you." "Don't lower your voice to me," snapped Hope. "I knew you when you were Louis Calhern."

After listening to Tallulah struggle through a song on a "Big

Show" broadcast, Jimmy Durante confided, "I think you ought to have your tonsils out." "I've already had them out," she replied. Durante suggested, "Then put 'em back in."

A guest at La Bankhead's Connecticut retreat was astonished when a servant brought him a glass of straight gin the moment he awoke. "Better drink it, darling," called Tallu from the next room. "I warn you there won't be another round served up before breakfast."

When Gypsy Rose Lee heard Tallulah Bankhead boast, "In all the years I've been on the stage, I never once forgot my lines," she scoffed, "What's so great about that? No audience ever forgot *mine.*"

Miss Lee once asked her doctor to vaccinate her where it wouldn't show. "Okay," agreed the doctor. "Stick out your tongue." Gypsy told her radio audience she was descended from a long line her mother once listened to. "Whenever I go out with a wolf, I think of her," added Miss Lee. "On the way home I suggest, 'Let's walk. I'm much too tired to ride in a taxi with you.' "

A new comedy act recorded a half-hour show on radio recently for submission to a big sponsor. "But there's no audience in the studio," complained one of the comedians. "How are we gonna get laughs?" The agent said, "Don't worry. We'll tape in laughs from a Groucho Marx recording." "But won't Groucho get sore?" persisted the comic. "Nah," the agent assured him. "He doesn't know it, but we taped in *his* laughs from Fred Allen." It was Allen, incidentally, who swore that he saw one Western film on TV so old that the cowboy was riding a dinosaur. "This new medium," adds Allen, "isn't a country-wide mania—yet, anyhow. There are still several states where they think Television is just a city in Israel."

A young co-ed looked dreamily at the ceiling and declared, "The man I marry must be an outstanding personality, be musical, tell new jokes, sing and dance, stay home, neither drink nor smoke, and shut up when I tell him to." Her caller arose, looked for his hat, and told her, "Lady, you don't want a husband; you want a television set."

Ken Murray noticed that one of the curvaceous redheads in the chorus of his television show was disgruntled and morose. "Oh, it isn't you, Mr. Murray," she hastened to explain. "It's this lug from Omaha I been showing the town to the last coupla weeks. Before he goes home, he gives me a coupla checks. And every one of them bounced back from the bank, stamped, 'Insufficient Fun'."

My pet aversions in radio and television at the moment are those ham actors who turn up endlessly on commercials in white surgical robes to report on complicated and dreary laboratory tests for dentifrices and cigarettes. And what's so wonderful, incidentally, about every cigarette being so mild nobody can even taste it? Maybe those sponsors are miscalculating the toughness of male smokers. I have a notion that the first cigarette maker who announces a brand that's so strong, pungent, and full-bodied it will knock your teeth out will sell a billion packs in two weeks.

Broadcaster Robert Trout had occasion to visit the dog pound one afternoon in Washington and was so touched by the plight of the mangy mongrels he saw there that he interpolated a plea into his newscast that night: every listener who mailed in a five-dollar bill would not only save the life of a defenseless dog, but would receive said dog for his very own. Some days later the director of the pound told Trout, "Did you slay them with that broadcast the other night! The five-dollar bills are still pouring in. In fact, they've arrived in such quantities, we've had to put on a dozen extra dog-catchers to satisfy the demand."

A political broadcast in Prague, says *Variety*, ended in wild cheers from the studio audience, followed by puzzling cries of "goal!" Next day the station manager apologized (before being carted off by the secret police). It seems the studio engineer had planned the usual "ovation" by getting a record from the files that carried the sound of prolonged applause. Unfortunately he made a slight mistake and selected one taken from the broadcast of a soccer game between Hungary and Czechoslovakia.

Herb Shriner, the greatest thing in homespun wits since the days of Will Rogers, spends a good deal of his time discussing the town drunk back in his Indiana birthplace. The poor fellow wasn't always that way; he simply took a nip now and then to "quiet his nerves." He finally quieted them so completely he couldn't move at all. "I don't even like the taste of the stuff," he confessed to Herb. "I just drink so's I can forget—and I got the best durn memory in Indiana." Herb suggested that he try leaving town, and he headed for the big town—Indianapolis. He was back in a week, however. "That place ain't for me," he announced. "I'll take the good old U.S.A."

Shriner, enlarging on an old Hoosier custom of passing a suit of clothes from father on through a succession of sons, recalls, "Often a feller in our town would find a suit had enough wear in it for a couple more kids, so he went right ahead and had 'em. A woman sure hated to see one of those durable suits come into the family. One lady finally stopped propagating because she was running out of names—to call her husband."

The richest citizen in Herb's town made his fortune in a novel manner. He invented a dog food that tastes exactly like a letter carrier's ankle. For years, says Herb, this character's watch has lacked an hour hand. He's waiting for something else to bust on it so's he can get the whole thing fixed at once.

Iced tea may be a cooling midsummer drink to most folks, but in Shriner's part of Indiana it's served exclusively in January, February, and March. "Those are the only months," he explains, "we have any ice." One worry the townsfolk have been spared. There's no traffic problem. "Lucky thing we don't need one-way streets," admits Herb. "There's only one street in town. If we made it one way, folks would just walk out of town and never be able to get back."

The camera crew and cast of a big television show trekked over to the wide open spaces of Jersey City recently to shoot a couple of sequences for a horse oprey. The story involved the flight of an ornery cattle thief over the Mexican border. The camera crew set up shop on one of the main New Jersey highways. The director found one stretch that had no buildings in view and had his technicians post a sign reading "Last gas station before the border. Twenty miles of uninhabited desert past this sign." By the time the director had rounded up his cast, he was dumfounded to discover a string of seventeen cars with out-of-state licenses lined up in front of his prop gas station. Although the towers of Newark were clearly visible ahead, these cautious drivers were taking no chances. They wanted their tanks full before braving those "twenty miles of uninhabited desert."

Myron Cohen tells about the Brooklyn kid who watched six wild West programs on TV every day. His mother sought one evening to lure him away from the machine and in to dinner, but the kid shot his pistol into the air and said, "Thanks, pard, but I reckon I ain't got any hankerin' tonight for matzoth balls."

Abe Burrows, embroiled in one of those television panel shows, was faced with the problem of guessing the identity of a mystery name. "Is he living?" asked Burrows hopefully. "No," said the quiz master. "He's dead." Burrows scratched his bald pate nervously and ruminated, "Let's see now. Who do I know who's dead?"

On a kids' quiz show, a radio M.C. asked a pimply-faced lad to name man's best friend—for two shiny silver dollars. When the lad hesitated the M.C. added a hint: "The word, sonny, begins with a 'D'." "Oh, yea," said the lad, brightening at once. "Dames!" And on *What's My Line,* Hal Block asked Rocky Graziano, "Are you a pugilist?" Rocky was lost in thought for a moment, then decided, "Nah—I'm just a prize-fighter."

A woebegone Casper Milquetoast asked M.C. Roger Price on a recent TV program, "How can I keep my wife from hanging around a bowling alley seven nights a week?" Price advised him tartly, "Get her a different job. Don't make her work as a pin-boy."

The new Television code sternly decrees, "No emphasis on anatomical details." Ben Gross, of the New York *News*, sought out Dagmar to ask, "What do you think of this provision?" "Honey," Dagmar assured him, "I don't need any emphasis."

T is for TEXAS—

And a Few Other States

Wall Street financier Arthur Goodman asked a Texas oil tycoon, "How's business holding up in your sector?" "Son," drawled the Texan, "in Houston we do more business by accident than you do in Wall Street on purpose." Later he admitted (in a much lower tone of voice), "If every boy in Texas, however, could read the mind of every girl in Texas, gas consumption in our state would drop off fifty per cent."

A Texas dowager presented herself at the Pearly Gates, and when Saint Peter asked for her credentials, proudly presented a membership card to the Symphony, receipted bills from Neiman-Marcus and the Shamrock Hotel, and a picture of herself shaking hands with Ted Dealey of the Dallas *News*. Saint Peter, duly impressed, remarked, "Come in, madam, by all means—but I don't think you'll like it."

Famous Dallas department store Neiman-Marcus had a visit from the wife of a multimillionaire oil tycoon. She wanted a new fur coat, and owner Stanley Marcus waited on her in person.

183

She inclined to a modest number that bore a price tag of exactly $32,000. Marcus told her, "We must warn everybody who picks out a coat of this particular fur that while it is very, very rare and uncommonly beautiful, it doesn't wear as well as, say, mink or sable, and may no longer look its best after two or three seasons. That being the case, I suppose you'll reconsider the purchase."

"On the contrary," said the customer promptly, "that being the case, I'd better have two of them!"

Vice-President Barkley was engaged in hot debate with one of those fabulous Texas oil millionaires over the merits of a neighboring Houstonian. "I'll bet he's as rich as you are," needled Barkley. "Don't let that fourflusher fool you," retorted the Texan angrily. "He's never had over thirty million dollars in his pocket at one time in his whole life."

A New Yorker was driving through a barren wilderness in West Texas when a fancy bird skittled past the car. "What kind of fowl do you call that?" he asked. The driver answered proudly, "That's a bird of paradise." "Hm-m-m," mused the New Yorker. "Kind of far from home, isn't he?"

Tony Martin, the man who made all America sing "Sole Mia," declares that Wichita Falls, Texas, is the only place in the world "where you can stand ankle-deep in mud and spit sand out of your mouth at the same time." He adds that they once had a dust storm so thick down there that a prairie dog was observed digging a hole fifty feet in the air.

An English visitor to Dallas, in a belittling mood, remarked, "You Texans don't do things as fast as I had been led to expect." "Zatso?" drawled Liz McMurray, the bookselling champion of the Southwest. "Just come down to Union Station with me and keep your eyes peeled." At the station, the superintendent was hurriedly drawing the redcaps into a single line. Just as the formation was completed, a streamliner whizzed by at a mile a minute. The Englishman got a fleeting glance at one passenger leaning out of a window with a notebook in his hand. "What was that chap trying to do?" demanded the Englishman. Answered Liz, "Just measuring the porters for new uniforms."

The Southern Methodist-Notre Dame football game was a sellout. Hordes of excited fans yelled their lungs out as the tide of fortune swayed now one way, now the other. And nobody yelled louder for SMU than a young priest who had a seat on the 35-yard line. During a time-out the man next to him admitted, "I can't figure, Father, why you are rooting for SMU. Surely you realize Notre Dame is a Catholic institution! How come?" The priest explained proudly, "First, suh, Ah am a Texan!"

Last year the Marine Historical Association at Mystic, Connecticut, enshrined the old ferry-boat *Brinckerhoff*—one of the last relics of the walking beam type—along the waterfront with other historic vessels like the whaleship *Charles W. Morgan* and the square-rigged *Joseph Conrad*. One canny visitor from New Hampshire stood before the ferry-boat, then shifted his gaze down-river towards the new highway bridge about half a mile away. His disparaging comment was, "Hmphh! Ferry-boat here, bridge there. The fools won't make a nickel!"

A boatman ran a ferry across a mountain stream full of whirl-pools and rapids. During a crossing in which the frail craft was tossed hither and yon by the swirling waters, a timid lady in the boat asked whether any passengers ever were lost in the river.

"Never," the boatman reassured her. "We always find them again the next day."

A Cleveland daily chronicles the visit of a Beacon Street Bos-tonite to a local belle which was marred by said belle's drawing on her gloves at the Cleveland Symphony. "In Boston," he told her severely, "men would as soon see a girl put on her girdle in public as her gloves." "In Cleveland," she informed him cheer-fully, "they'd rather."

A lady from Beacon Hill in Boston was taken to a session of the U.N. When she got home friends asked her what it was like. "Dreadful," said the lady. "It was simply crawling with foreign-ers!"

There's a neat twist in this story of Sam Levenson's. A cloak and suit manufacturer, obviously born abroad, was taunted on his Americanism by a bigoted blue-blood. "What kind of Ameri-can are you, after all?" sneered the blue-blood. "Why, my ances-tors came over on the Mayflower." The cloak and suit man, un-perturbed, replied, "Maybe it's lucky they did. By the time I arrived, the immigration laws were a lot stricter."

George Allen's Uncle John spent most of his declining days on his Mississippi plantation fighting over the battles of the Civil

War. One week-end, however, he journeyed to Washington on business, and was approached by a battered wreck of a man who begged for aid. Every scar and blemish, the panhandler declared, had been sustained while fighting bravely on the Union side. To Allen's amazement, Uncle John promptly coughed up a five-dollar bill, explaining to his nephew, "That was the first damyankee I ever saw shot up to my entire satisfaction."

In a local election in Mississippi, officials tabulating the ballots were astounded to discover a Republican vote. There being no precedent for this phenomenon, the sheriff decided, "Let's hold it out till we get a full count." Then—wonder of wonders!—another Republican vote turned up. "That settles it," roared the sheriff. "The low-down varmint voted twice, so we won't count either of them."

A Nashville lady put down her paper with a sigh and reflected, "To think a Southern boy could go so far wrong." The old girl in the adjoining rocking chair, startled by the Nashville lady's vehemence, exclaimed, "I do declare, Mary Lou! What Southern boy are you runnin' down?" "That Joe Stalin," pouted the Nashville lady. "You know, of course, he's from Georgia."

Father Edward Murphy, a wise and witty Catholic priest in New Orleans, and an implacable foe of racial intolerance, tells of an old colored man who drove his dilapidated jalopy through a red light on Canal Street. Arrested and taken before a judge, the old man explained, "Yo' honor, Ah saw all the white folks goin' through the green light, so Ah jus' went through the red." "The case was dismissed," adds Father Murphy.

Emmet Dedmon tells about a book salesman who was selling his line to a dealer in the deep, deep South. "Our next novel," said the salesman with an apologetic cough, "deals with the problem of—er, incest." "That's the trouble with you Yankees," snapped the dealer. "You make a problem out of everything."

A familiar character on Wall Street some years ago was a colorful broker named Pop Schwed. Pop loved nothing better than to reel off apocryphal tales of his youth in the wide-open town of Goldfield, Nevada, just after the turn of the century. There was one hellion there, he recalled, who went berserk every time he had six drinks inside of him, which was *usually*. An itinerant medico persuaded him that if he didn't forswear all hard liquor at once he'd be dead inside two months. One evening the reformed character was in the toughest dive in Goldfield, disconsolately sipping a beaker of ginger ale, when a prospector sashayed to the bar, pumped his faithless wife and her paramour full of lead, shot out the lights as a parting gesture, and vanished into the night. The paralyzed silence that followed was finally broken by Pop Schwed's reformed friend. "Waiter," he barked hoarsely, "for God's sake! A double order of ham and eggs!"

A couple who never before had ventured west of Hoboken were making their first transcontinental trip aboard a Canadian streamliner. At one stop far along the line they left the train for a little exercise, and inquired of a man on the platform, "What's the name of this town?" He answered, "Sascatoon, Saskatchewan." "Goodness," marveled the husband, "we've come so far the natives don't even speak English here!"

Harry Oliver, editor of *The Desert Rat* (a newspaper published four times a year) swears that an Indian strode into a white man's court and pleaded to have his name shortened legally. "What's your name now?" asked the judge. "Chief Train-whistle," said the Indian. "And what do you want to shorten it to?" pursued the judge. The Indian folded his arms majestically and grunted, "Toots."

Oliver once persuaded a honeymoon couple headed for Yellowstone Park that the whole thing was a fake. "Those geysers gave out years ago," he assured them. "The government secretly installed underground boilers with time clocks and pressure gauges. They couldn't stand the thought of losing all that tourist revenue. They even bring out those mangy bears every summer from zoos in the east." The honeymooners were so outraged they changed their plans and went to Reno instead.

In their colorful memoir, *Trail Driving Days*, Dee Brown and Martin Schmitt recall a wild night in a saloon in Mingusville, South Dakota, back in 1885. A Bad Lands drunk had just shot up the premises and sent the bartender to cover behind the counter when he spied a bespectacled tenderfoot minding his own business at a rear table. The drunk announced boldly, "Four-Eyes will now set up drinks for the house." Four-Eyes turned slowly, and after two shots from the drunk went wild, knocked him senseless with a single punch to the solar plexus. After that Tenderfoot Rancher Theodore Roosevelt was affectionately known in those parts as "Old Four-Eyes."

Those were the days, add Brown and Schmitt, when the wildest town of all was Dodge City. When a liquored-up cowhand boarded a Santa Fe local one afternoon and demanded a ride to hell, the conductor suggested, "Give me two dollars fare and get off at Dodge."

If just a little of the rainfall that beats down so persistently on the coastal region of Washington and Oregon could be transferred to the bone-dry areas of lower California and Arizona not so many hundred miles to the south, it would be a wonderful deal all around. One day you're listening to a Southwestern farmer praying for any kind of shower to break a seven-month drought; the next a University of Washington professor is saying, "That majestic peak about sixty miles to the southeast is Mount Rainier, of course. I use it as a weather guide every morning. If I can see it when I awaken I know it's going to rain later in the day. If I can't see it I know it's raining already!" When Seattle folk *can* see Mount Rainier or when Mount Hood is visible to the citizens of Portland, incidentally, the common phrase is "Oh, look: the mountain is out today."

The cause of all the rain is the Japan Current, which warms the air blowing in from the Pacific. The warm air turns into rain when it collides with the formidable Cascade Range.

"The far ends of the earth" is an empty phrase today. As Willis Brown points out, there is no spot on the globe in 1952 that is theoretically more than forty hours' flying time from your nearest airport!

U is for
UNIVERSITIES

Albert Einstein, whose theories about relativity and the fourth dimension are said to be understood by only twelve people in the world besides himself, graciously allowed a film producer to take some shots for a documentary movie in his Princeton, N.J., residence not long ago.

Left alone momentarily in the library, the producer noticed a big blueprint on Dr. Einstein's desk.

Since he himself was having a new house built at the time, and had blueprints coming out of his ears, he felt an uncontrollable impulse to have a look at the Einsteinian conception.

Unable to make head or tail of it, he looked for the legend in the lower right-hand corner. Immaculately lettered, it read, "One inch equals a hundred million light years."

Money means little to Dr. Einstein. When he first joined the Princeton Institute for Advanced Study, the salary he requested was so low officials had to double it to preserve some semblance of Institute standards.

He once used a $1500 check from the Rockefeller Foundation as a bookmark, then lost the book. The Foundation's records were out of kilter for months. When they finally sent a duplicate check, Einstein wrote back, "What's this for?"

Orpah Anderson tells me this happened at a school in a northern Minnesota town. A strapping, healthy-looking girl appeared to register for a course in English. The recording clerk asked, "Have you a hobby?" The girl replied, "No, ay ban single."

Donald Clark quotes a Columbia professor's appraisal of a high-flying colleague: "Such time as he can spare from the adornment of his person, he devotes to the neglect of his profession."

The University of Michigan prides itself on the exchange students it attracts from every corner of the world. One day some delegates from the Far East arrived unexpectedly at the Ann Arbor station clad in white suits with turbans wound around their heads. The station master called up then-President Ruthven and asked, "What'll I do with them? They don't seem to understand the questions I ask them. Only one speaks any English." "Send the one who speaks English to my office and hold the others till you hear from me," instructed Dr. Ruthven. In due course the emissary who "spoke English" arrived before Dr. Ruthven, bowed low, and gravely began, "Sir or madam, whichever the case may be . . ."

Gargoyle, the humorous magazine at Michigan, is one campus publication that isn't devoting all its efforts to unsuccessful imitations of the *New Yorker*. In the issue I saw, the cartoons were raucous and uninhibited; the jokes had that well-remembered tang of typical undergraduate wit. Examples: She: I saw a Texas Ranger carrying two rifles. He: That's nothing. I saw a cowgirl packing a pair of 38's. . . . Didja hear about the pregnant bedbug? It's going to have a baby in the spring. . . . Girl: I nearly fainted when the fellow I was out with last night asked me for a kiss. Boy: Baby, you're gonna die when you hear what I have to say. . . . Sam: What did the usherette say when her strap broke? Ed: I dunno. What did she say? Sam: I have two down in front.

Two collegians had celebrated their team's football triumph too copiously, and were driving home at midnight in rather erratic fashion. For miles, their road paralleled the tracks of the Chicago and Northwestern Railroad. Suddenly a passenger train rumbled by them going in the opposite direction. The driver commented, "Didja notice that every house in that village we just passed was still lit up?" "Not only that," added his passenger, "but the first house was on fire."

Ohio State University once invited a distinguished old judge to speak at a convocation. They didn't realize that the gentleman, always eccentric, had grown worse with the years, and was somewhat senile into the bargain. He seized his typescript firmly, plodded up to the lectern, and began reading in a high, cracked voice. When he got to the bottom of Page One, he turned the leaf, and continued reading. It soon became apparent to the startled audience that the judge was rereading Page One. And if that wasn't enough, the third page was another duplicate!

By this time, everybody realized that the typist had delivered the judge's speech in triplicate. Seventeen pages were read three times over by the unsuspecting old gentleman. The chairman then rushed out for an aspirin, and the audience rushed out to have hysterics.

The father of every candidate for admission to Vassar is required to fill out a questionnaire regarding his daughter's qualifications. One of the questions is "Would you call your daughter a leader?" A father in Red Bank, New Jersey, meticulously honest, answered, "I have never noticed my daughter assume the role of leader, but I do know she is an excellent follower." Vassar's reply, as reported by the *Journal of Education,* was, "As our freshman group next fall seems to be composed almost exclusively of several hundred leaders, we congratulate ourselves that your daughter will also be a member of the class. We shall thus be assured of one good follower, at any rate. Her application is approved with enthusiasm."

"Did your girl like the Bikini bathing suit you brought her from Paris?" asked Williams, '53. "Did she!" enthused Williams, '52. "She tried it on immediately—and you should have seen her beam."

The dean of one Midwestern seat of learning was leading the robed group of notables and faculty members across the campus to Commencement ceremonies in the quadrangle when he stole a glance at his watch, made a mental calculation, and suddenly wheeled to the left. The procession wheeled after him, and solemnly followed him en masse—to the gents' room!

Another dean suffered the misfortune of sitting down on a newly painted bench just before graduation exercises began. He turned disaster into triumph, however, by opening his remarks with, "I had hoped to bring you an unvarnished tale this morning, but fate decreed otherwise."

"Why did you assault this poor man?" a judge demanded of a college student near the tag-end of a football week-end. "Well, judge," explained the student, wriggling in the grasp of the cop who had haled him into court, "I was in a phone booth innocently conversing with my girl when this bohunk opens the door and heaves me out of the booth." "And that incensed you?" prompted the judge. "Mildly," admitted the student, "but what really made me see red was when he reached in for my girl and heaved her out, too."

Mingling with the throng that poured out of a California university stadium after a big game, a visiting Easterner enthused to his host, head of the chemistry department, "What a plant you have here! What a campus! How many students would you say you have?" The chemistry prof answered sourly, "About one in a thousand."

Two sweet co-eds at the University of Minnesota were happily carving up an ex-roommate over the telephone. "And, my dear," continued one, "who do you think she's been dating like mad the past month? Her X-ray specialist!" "Hmphh!" commented the other. "I wonder what he sees in her?"

Professor Irwin Edman, famed for his absent-mindedness, dropped in unexpectedly on his old friend, the family doctor, and chatted happily about his impending trip to France for almost three hours. Finally the doctor arose from his chair, and remarked pointedly, "Well, Irwin, I have an operation to perform at eight

in the morning. I trust everyone in your household is well."
"Good heavens," gasped Irwin, "that reminds me. I came here to
tell you my cook is having a fit."

V is for

VIPS IN WASHINGTON

Presidents come and go, but the shenanigans designed to charm the voters remain about the same. A delegation from the west, come to visit Teddy Roosevelt in Oyster Bay, for example, found him striding out of the house in a pair of levis, with a pitchfork in his hand. "You can talk to me while I work, gentlemen. I've raised some bully hay this season. James, where's that hay of mine?"

Back came the voice of James: "Sorry, Mr. President, but I just ain't had time to replace it since you forked it up for yesterday's contingent!"

Woodrow Wilson was a great reader of books, and the author he admired above all others was Mark Twain. When his presidential train passed through Hannibal, Missouri, therefore, Mr. Wilson ordered a three-hour wait-over that he might wander for a bit among the boyhood haunts of the famous humorist. Accosting a native, the President said, "I'm a stranger in these parts. Could you tell me where Tom Sawyer was supposed to live?" "Never heard of him," maintained the native. "Well, how about Huck Finn?" persisted Mr. Wilson. "Never heard of him nuther," declared the native. The President made one more try. "How about Puddinhead Wilson?" he inquired. The native's face brightened.

197

"I heard of him all right," he said cheerfully. "In fact, I even voted for the durn fool."

When Cal Coolidge was President, he liked to raid the icebox occasionally for a late snack, and generally took Colonel Starling, his Secret Service man, with him. Coolidge usually whipped up two sandwiches of Vermont cheese.

"That cheese," says Starling, "was as strong as a billy goat. Mr. Coolidge would turn to me and exclaim, 'I'll bet no other President of the United States ever made a cheese sandwich for you.' 'No,' I would answer. 'It's a great honor.' Coolidge would add gloomily, 'I have to furnish the cheese, too.'"

When Ex-President Herbert Hoover was an undergraduate at Stanford, he served a spell as manager of the baseball team. One day Benjamin Harrison, himself just retired from the Presidency of the United States, tried to get into a game without a ticket. He didn't get by Herbert Hoover! In fact, he ended up by buying another ticket in advance for the next week's game. "That," recalls Mr. Hoover, "was my first contact with a great public man." He acted with similar dispatch and decisiveness when he found himself shepherding hundreds of stranded Americans in London in 1914. One heedless debutante from Lansing, Michigan, went right on collecting a $5000 trousseau despite the crisis, and, since she no longer trusted any foreigners, had every parcel delivered in care of the Hoovers at the Savoy Hotel. Just as promptly as a package arrived, the hastily assembled Hoover committee turned it over to some unfortunate whose entire baggage had been lost in the confusion. The debutante's father cabled he would sue for damages. Mr. Hoover invited him by a collect return cable to come and try it.

Another casualty of those hectic August, 1914, days was a twelve-year-old American kid who was sent along to visit his grandparents in Croatia, and when war broke out was stranded, helpless, in Hamburg. By great good fortune, however, he ran into the fully accoutred members of a wild West show, and promptly attached himself to the troupe. By the time they reached London, the kid was determined that his future lay in show business. His father cabled Mr. Hoover to make sure he was in good hands and bound for home. "Stop worrying," advised Mr. Hoover. "Your boy is headed for America under the excellent charge of Chief White Feather, of Pawhuska, Oklahoma."

Ex-President Herbert Hoover vacationed recently in a small Canadian resort. The clerk examined his signature in the register, and was obviously impressed. "Any relation of G-Man Hoover?" he asked. When Mr. Hoover said no, he tried again. "How about the Hoover who makes those vacuum cleaners?" Again Ex-President Hoover said no. "Oh, well," consoled the clerk. "No harm done. We do get a kick, though, out of entertaining relatives of real celebrities!"

There is no bee with a more virulent or lasting bite than the presidential bee. Once a man gets stung by it, he's never quite the same again as long as he lives. It was Mrs. Franklin D. Roosevelt who told me that at Hyde Park, and she added with a smile, "I'm the girl who ought to know." Paul McNutt, who campaigned actively for a while for the Democratic nomination in 1940, once answered an inquiring reporter, "Would I like to be President? Lady, there have been moments when I wanted to be President so bad my teeth ached."

Just before the balloting began in the 1940 Republican Convention, recalls Stefan Lorant, the late Wendell Willkie sought to enlist the support of crusty delegate Jim Watson of Indiana. "Sorry, Wendell," snapped Watson, "but you're just not my kind of dependable, day-in-and-day-out Republican." "I am now," maintained Mr. Willkie, "though I admit I once was a Democrat." "Once was?" snorted Watson. "Well, let me tell you what I think of converts. If a fancy woman truly repented and wanted to join my church, I'd welcome her with open arms. I'd even lead her personally to the front pew. But by the eternal, I wouldn't ask her to lead the choir!"

No President was the subject of more jibes and anecdotes than Harry S. Truman. Like him or not, one had to admire the unfailing good nature with which he greeted them—at least, in public. He himself retold the one, for instance, about the three most disastrous occurrences in our history: the Galveston Flood, the San Francisco Earthquake, and the failure of a certain haberdashery in Kansas City. There was another about a Californian who remarked to a man from Houston that he heard Truman was going to raise taxes. With no further ado, the Houstonian arose, and knocked the visitor cold with an uppercut to the jaw. A friend protested, "What did you want to do that for to a man who merely said 'Truman's going to raise taxes'?" "Is *that* what he said?" mumbled the Houstonian, his face flushing with embarrassment. "I thought he said 'Truman was *raised in Texas*'!"

Then there was Walter Richards' story of the day during the 1948 Presidential campaign when Mr. Truman's train stopped on an Indian reservation and the President emerged to deliver a speech. "I am appalled," he said, "at the treatment of you noble redmen and women by administrations previous to mine, particularly the Republicans." He made a gesture as though he was chopping a Republican in the neck and continued, "As our train pulled in, I saw squaws washing clothes by the riverside, pummeling them on rocks, even as your ancestors did. I intend to see a Bendix installed in every teepee!"

The Indians broke into loud cries of "Oompah-oompah!"

The President beamed broadly and continued, "And I understand you are still obliged to dry beef for jerky. Well, I intend to see that every wigwam is equipped with a deep freeze."

Again the Indians shouted "Oompah-oompah!"

The President broke into his broadest grin and soared to a climax. "If re-elected I intend to see that your noble chief drives a Cadillac as big as mine, and a new Pontiac shall stand before every teepee."

As he bowed, the Indians roared out their mightiest "Oompah" and their handsome chief came forward and placed a war bonnet on the President's head. Then he led the Great White Father to the corrals for another presentation, delivering the speech in the impeccable English of a Carlyle graduate. "The Indians of this reservation take great pleasure in presenting as a token of our esteem a silver-mounted saddle and our very best Indian pony." As the President prepared to mount the handsome animal, the Chief suddenly cried out, "Be careful, Mr. Truman. Don't step in the oompah!"

There's a sign on the bulletin board of the Clinton, Ky., school where Alben Barkley earned spending money in his youth as assistant janitor. It reads, "Al Barkley swept here."

Warns an English diplomat: "If you aspire to be a statesman today, you'd better watch your appease and accuse."

In general, United States senators try to agree and disagree with a certain amount of moderation and decorum, but every

once in a while there have been explosions on the floor that did
not stop short of fisticuffs.

After one such violent outburst, a senator from Vermont had
worked himself up to such a state that occupants of the Visitors'
Gallery distinctly heard him mutter to himself as he stomped off
the floor:

"I'm going home to dinner. If it's ready, I won't eat it. If it
isn't, I'll raise hell!"

A Texas Democrat had successfully campaigned for a seat in
the House of Representatives. To show his appreciation, he
promptly introduced a bill to finance the widening of Trinity
River back home. A Republican congressman from up north
jumped to his feet in indignation.

"What can the government do for a piddling trickle like the
Trinity?" he demanded. "Why, I can spit halfway acrost it." The
Speaker of the House banged with his gavel and cried, "You're
out of order." "You're damn right, I'm out of order," agreed the
Republican. "If I was in order, I could spit all the way acrost it."

Every politician, suggests Carl Sandburg, should have three
hats handy at all times: one for throwing into the ring, another
for talking through, and a third for pulling rabbits out of if
elected!

A staunch Republican from Maine was being shown the wonders of the Grand Canyon. "Yes, sir," said the guide. "It took
about five million years for this awe-inspiring canyon to be carved
out of the rocks." "Hmm," added the man from Maine. "Government project, I presume."

A congressman's wife sought the advice of a "K" Street fortune-teller, who prophesied, "Prepare yourself for widowhood! Your husband is about to die a violent death."

The wife sighed deeply and asked, "Will I be acquitted?"

In Detroit, a seven-year-old protégé of Harvey Campbell's held up a picture of Abraham Lincoln and gravely declared, "This is the man who frayed the sleeves." "You're a bit off the beam," explained Harvey. "Mr. Lincoln is the man who freed the slaves. The President who frayed the sleeves didn't come along until many years later."

Country-wide scandals in the internal revenue department led one businessman to declare, "I'm all ready to pay the current installment on my income tax, but I don't know what jail to mail the check to." . . . Joe Eckhouse, handsome department-store executive, classifies the Eiffel Tower as "The Empire State Building after taxes." . . . A Cabinet member pleading for still higher taxes was taken apart by a syndicated gossip columnist. A reporter asked him, "How do you classify gossip columnists, sir? Would you call them newspapermen?" The Cabinet member snorted, "Would you call barnacles ships?"

It's unlikely that a certain Senator's wife will be wearing to any more public functions a medallion her husband picked up for her on an air junket to Hong Kong. She was very proud of it for quite a while—until the evening, in fact, that a Chinese Nationalist diplomat, over to address the U.N., informed her gravely that the literal translation of the Chinese characters on the medallion read, "Licensed prostitute, City of Shanghai."

Preparing to attend a banquet given by Gwendolyn Cafritz, now Washington's number-one hostess, a Senator from a Rocky Mountain state slipped on the top step of a marble staircase and landed solidly on his posterior two floors below. The next morning he called from his bed of pain to apologize to the famous hostess.

"You're forgiven," she said, "but you ruined my seating arrangement." "*Your* seating arrangement," he exclaimed. "You ought to see *mine!*"

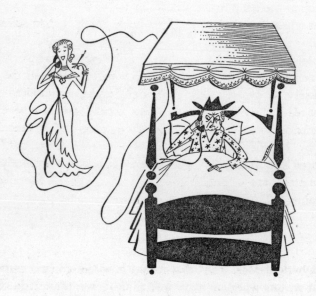

W is for
WRITERS

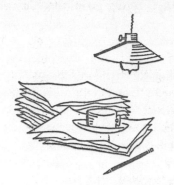

Only one man in a million dares to make a living by draping live hooded cobras around his neck, and there was a notable sparsity of volunteers for the job of riveting that new television mast to the top of the Empire State Building.

Yet when it comes to writing a book—a job that in some ways is infinitely harder to master than that of any snake charmer or steeplejack every man, woman, child, prison inmate, illiterate and confirmed lunatic firmly believes he possesses all the talent necessary. A typical note accompanying an unsolicited manuscript reads, "My friends have insisted that I simply *must* put my experiences into a book. Please mail contracts and advance royalties by Monday as the landlord is getting impatient." Nine hundred and ninety-nine out of every thousand manuscripts, unfortunately, are unpublishable. Nine hundred of them are unreadable.

Playwright Moss Hart discovered how the general public felt about writers when he journeyed to the lower East Side of Manhattan in search of local color for a script he is preparing. Picking his way through the maze of pushcarts and pedestrians on Hester Street, he suddenly heard his name being called.

The voice belonged to the proprietor of one of the pushcarts, who cackled, "Well, well, Moss, I recognized you immediately! Don't you remember me? Goldberg? We sat next to each other in public school in the Bronx." "Oh, yes! Goldberg . . ." repeated Hart uncertainly, while the pushcart man continued pounding him vehemently on the back and inquired, "What are you doing for a living?" "I write," answered the playwright. "Write what?" said the man. "Oh, plays and movies and things like that," explained Hart. Goldberg was fascinated.

"I don't want to get personal," he declared, "but what did you make from this, say, in the year 1950?"

Hart calculated, "I'd say it was in the neighborhood of $250,000." Goldberg shot a contemptuous look at his pushcart, clapped a hand to his forehead and exclaimed, "$250,000! From *writing?* Why couldn't I have thought of that?"

Elliot Paul, author of *Springtime in Paris,* cherishes as his favorite memory the time his then-publisher, the late Horace Liveright, mailed back the manuscript of *The Governor of Massachusetts* and told him to cut 10,000 words. Paul kept it a week, returned it without opening the package. Liveright wired, "Congratulations. Now it's perfect!"

Occasionally a writer comes along who can sit down at a typewriter and bang out a column or story at will. Most writers, however, can think of more ways to delay getting down to their work than even a temporary kitchen maid. Lee Rogow cites the case of one Hollywood scenario scripter who simply had to have a job completed by the following morning. His understanding wife disconnected the phone, inserted a fresh page in his typewriter, grabbed both kids by the hand and left him in sole possession of the premises. They rode to the end of the bus line and back, saw a double feature at the neighborhood movie, and came home at the tag end of the day to see how far Daddy had gotten. He hadn't done too badly. As they walked though the door, he was just polishing the last piece of their eighty-piece sterling-silver dinner set.

In his uninhibited and engrossing autobiography, William Carlos Williams, who is at one time a prize-winning poet and one of the busiest small-town physicians in New Jersey, gives the following report of the first time Marcel Proust met James Joyce:

Rabid partisans had placed two chairs side by side in the middle of the room. There the two heroes seated themselves, and everybody waited for the wits to sparkle and flash. Joyce said, "I have headaches every day. My eyes are terrible." Proust replied, "With me, it's my poor stomach. What am I going to do? It's killing me. In fact, I must leave at once." "I'm in the same situation," declared Joyce, rising, "if I can find someone to take me by the arm and get me out of here. Good-by." Proust's exit line was "Charmé. Oh, my stomach, my stomach!"

My own first meeting with James Joyce was on the spectacular side. I found him in Sylvia Beach's Paris bookshop with one arm in a sling, a bandaged foot propped up on a stool and a patch over one eye. Noting my dismay, Miss Beach hastened to assure me, "Don't think he always looks this way. He's been run over twice this week by taxicabs!"

Humorist Stephen Leacock had a long string of college degrees, and Canadian associates usually addressed him as "Doctor." The purser of an Atlantic liner, who had heard him thus referred to for three days, stepped up to him one evening and said, "Doctor, could I prevail upon you to examine the star of last year's Ziegfeld Follies? She slipped on the promenade deck and I'm afraid she has sprained her hip." Leacock reported ruefully

later, "I rushed there like a startled gazelle, but alas! two doctors
of divinity had beaten me to it."

An author preparing an article on censorship unearthed the
following interesting facts: In 1885 Concord, Massachusetts,
home town of Thoreau, banned *Huckleberry Finn* as "trash suitable only for the slums." In 1929 Russia blacklisted Sherlock
Holmes for his "disgraceful occultism and spiritualism." In 1931
China banned *Alice in Wonderland* on the ground that "animals
should not use human language" and that it was "disastrous to put
animals and human beings on the same level."

During Mark Twain's reporting days in Virginia City, fame
and fortune were still very much in the future. The wife of the
owner of a big silver mine met him on C Street one day with a
cigar box held tightly under his arm. "Mr. Twain," she reproached
him, "you promised me you were going to give up smoking
cigars." "Madam," replied Twain with great dignity, "this box
does not contain cigars. I am moving my possessions from one
abode to another."

Twain, says Vincent Starrett, once visited the celebrated
Madame Tussaud's wax works in London, and was admiring a
replica of Queen Victoria when he felt a sudden stab of pain in
his posterior. Wheeling angrily, he found himself face to face with
a flabbergasted British matron, her umbrella still pointed at him.
"O lor', it's alive!" she gasped, and fled into the night.

Amy Lowell, famed American poetess, sold her first effort to a
national magazine at the age of six. The editor quoted the letter
she had written to accompany the poem. It concluded with the

eye-opening sentence, "I have always been a loving son to my father, Augustus Lowell." When her father inquired, "Why on earth did you refer to yourself as my 'son'?" Amy replied, "Because I couldn't spell 'daughter.'"

When Danny Kaye made a great hit in James Thurber's *Walter Mitty,* Producer Sam Goldwyn thought he'd like to have Thurber as a permanent addition to his writing stable. The catch lay in the fact that Thurber was working very happily for the late *New Yorker* Editor Harold Ross and had no desire whatever to dally further with picture-making. "I'll pay you five hundred dollars a week," wrote Goldwyn. "Sorry," answered Thurber after some delay, "but Mr. Ross has met the increase." Goldwyn thereupon raised the ante to a thousand, then fifteen hundred, and finally twenty-five hundred a week, but each time got nothing for his pains but the courteous response, "Mr. Ross has met the increase." There followed a long interim of silence. Then one day Mr. Goldwyn wrote again. This time, for some unknown reason, his offer went down to fifteen hundred. Thurber wrote back, "I'm sorry, but Mr. Ross has met the decrease."

There will never be an editor more sorely missed than the same Harold Ross, who founded the *New Yorker* in 1925, and guided it unerringly until his death in 1951. A fastidious and impeccable craftsman at all times, Ross in personal life was a cranky, untidy curmudgeon, whose wild gestures, tousled hair, and rasping voice made him stand out like a sore thumb in all literary and social conclaves. After a row with him, Dorothy Parker once exclaimed, "When the revolution comes, it will be everybody in the world against Harold Ross!" Ross himself referred to his more irascible moments as "those times I went crazy." After hiring a promising lad who sought a place on the staff, Ross assured him, "Don't be too pleased with yourself. I hire any blank blank fool who sticks his face in here." Then he added, "Don't think you're going to start as a reporter. You'll begin as managing editor just like everybody else." One of the last things Ross told his staff was, "From now on I flatly refuse to buy one more story I don't understand." With all his roaring and grumbling, however, Ross left more friends behind, more writers and artists seriously saddened by his death, than any other editor in recent years.

Appointments mean little in the life of Budd Schulberg, talented but vague author of *What Makes Sammy Run?* and *The Disenchanted*. The blare of a be-bop band or the sound of a padded glove against a punching bag will distract him from a scheduled conference, with a fifty-thousand-dollar movie contract at stake. He was leaving for a formal dinner party in New York one day when the maid at his Bucks County farm asked him to deliver a dachshund pup to a friend who ran a beauty shop in Harlem. Budd, intrigued with the mission, promptly forgot the dinner party. He also forgot his driver's license—and the address of the lady who ran the beauty shop. At two the next morning I was awakened by a phone call from the lieutenant at the Harlem police precinct. "We picked up a fellow driving aimlessly around

Harlem without a license," he told me indignantly. "Says he's an author of yours. Says, too, he's trying to deliver a dachshund. At two in the morning, mind you! I hate to bother you with a cock-and-bull story like that . . ." "Wait a minute," I interrupted, "that must be Budd Schulberg, and it's perfectly all right. He does things like that. He's also the author of *What Makes Sammy Run?*" The baffled lieutenant settled for an autographed copy.

An author offered a publisher a sensational biography of a promi-nent Broadway personage. "It's full of dynamite," agreed the pub-lisher, "but I'll have to have my lawyer check it carefully for libel." "That won't be necessary," said the author. "Every story I use in the book was told to me by somebody!"

Clyde Beck, erudite Detroit editor, presided at a dinner in honor of bibliophile John Winterich recently. Mr. Beck informed a large and enthusiastic gathering, "Our guest this evening needs no introduction," which was a lucky break, all things considered, because at this point Mr. Beck lost his balance and fell off the speaker's platform. Winterich restored order by assuring his audience, "Mr. Beck is an improvement in one respect. The last fellow who introduced me at a dinner suffered a heart attack."

At the conclusion of an Authors' League meeting, a group of distinguished men of letters repaired to the coffee shop of a mid-town hotel for a late snack. One of the authors inadvertently knocked over the salt. Being superstitious, he quickly threw a handful over his left shoulder to ward off bad luck. A young waitress was bending over the table to distribute portions of scrambled eggs, and the salt went straight down the back of her dress.

She wriggled impatiently, put down the tray to scratch herself, and remarked tartly, "Nothing doing, big boy. You won't get me that way!"

One of the most improbable anecdotes about the late George Bernard Shaw concerns an evening when a lady dramatist horn-swoggled him into attending the tryout of her new play. "Now, you naughtly man," she chided kittenishly, "you're not to sneak out in the middle of my drama." Shaw was planked down behind her and leaned forward to get a better view of the proceedings. Halfway through the first act, the authoress felt a tickling sensation on her neck. Groping in the dark, she felt a loose strand of hair and tucked it firmly into place with a big hatpin. Suddenly Shaw, thoroughly bored by this time, decided to fall back in his seat. He cried, "Ouch!" Then he told the authoress, "Madam, if you will kindly take my beard out of your hair, I promise I won't budge out of this seat until your confounded play is over."

W (and X, Y, and Z) are for
WOMEN

A long-time inmate of a Displaced Persons camp finally got his visa and sailed off for America, faithfully promising to send for his wife the moment he achieved a respectable bank balance. Unfortunately, he forgot all about her until he received a letter from her some six months later. Unable to read, he persuaded the neighborhood butcher to divulge the letter's contents to him. The butcher, who had a voice like a foghorn on the *Queen Elizabeth*, opened the letter and read hoarsely, "Why haven't you sent for me? I need some money right away. Minnie."

The immigrant snatched the note from the butcher's hands, stuffed it angrily into his pocket and forgot about it until a month later when he found himself dining with a gentle young rabbi. Again he asked, "Will you read my wife's letter to me, please?" This time it was the soft, modulated voice of the rabbi that echoed, "Why haven't you sent for me? I need some money right away. Minnie." The immigrant nodded with satisfaction. "Anyhow," he remarked, "I'm glad to notice that she's changed her tone!"

The advertising manager of a big Chicago daily has decided that women are like newspapers, reports *Tide*, and lists the fol-

lowing reasons to support his thesis: They have forms; they are
made up; they have bold types; they always have the last word;
they have great influence; they carry news wherever they go;
they are much thinner than they used to be; and finally, every
man should have one of his own and not borrow his neighbor's.
The manager adds this postscript: Back numbers are not in demand.

A long-suffering husband took one look at his huge pile of un-
paid bills for the month and reached for the family shotgun. "I'm
going to end it all," he threatened. His wife remained totally un-
impressed.

"Put down that gun before it goes off by accident," she ordered.
"If you have something to say, shut up!"

Phil Silvers, in *Top Banana*, mourns, "Ever since the honeymoon, my wife has been hitting the ceiling. What a lucky thing
for me she's such a rotten shot!"

Neal O'Hara visited an old pal whose equanimity was upset by
his wife's dramatic announcement that she was so sick of wearing
old rags she had marched into Filene's that afternoon and bought
ten new dresses. "Ten!" shrieked the wounded husband. "What
could any dame want with ten new dresses?" The wife answered
promptly, "Ten new hats."

"I'm getting mighty exhausted contesting my wife's will," admitted Mr. Hecubar to a confidante. "I never knew she had died,"

said the shocked confidante. "That's the trouble," sighed Mr. Hecubar. "She didn't."

A woman stalked into the office of the head of a private detective agency and demanded an interview. Before the startled head of the firm could say a word, the woman launched into a tirade against her husband. Finally, when she stopped to get her breath, the detective was able to get a word in.

"Just what do you want me to do, madam?" he asked.

"I want my husband and that woman followed," snapped the visitor. "I want them followed night and day, and then I want a complete report on what she sees in him."

A fantastically henpecked husband finally did something entirely on his own initiative. He dropped dead. His nagging wife mourned his loss—and the fact that she had nobody left to badger. A visitor sympathized, "How you must miss dear Wilbur." "Yes," said the widow wistfully, "it seems but yesterday that he stood at that very door, holding it open until two flies got in."

In the powder room of a Cambridge residence, Mrs. Cabot-Lodge preened herself and said loftily, "That South African gentleman says the nicest things! He remarked particularly on my birdlike appetite." "Hmmph," commented Mrs. Lowellstall. "He runs an ostrich farm!"

Sam Himmell writes about a new millionaire in Scarsdale who was showing a friend around his modernistic "push-button" mansion. "This is the best gadget of the lot," he exulted. "After a

night out, I sometimes feel like stepping into a nice hot bath right here without the trouble of going into the bathroom. I just press this button——" He pressed the button and in rolled the bathtub, full of nice hot water—and the millionaire's wife.

An upstate social leader was expecting a large group of friends at her home one evening, and knowing her husband's propensity for using guest towels indiscriminately when he returned from the office, put a sign on the ones she had trotted out especially for the occasion that read, "If you use one of these towels, I'll slay you in cold blood." Unfortunately, she forgot to remove the note before the guests started arriving. At the evening's end she found the note still there—and not one towel touched.

Erskine lounged into the office an hour late for the third time in one week and found the boss awaiting him, arms akimbo. "What's the story this time, Erskine?" he asked sarcastically. "Let's hear a good excuse for a change." Erskine sighed, "Everything went wrong this morning, boss. The wife decided to drive me to the station. She got ready in ten minutes, but then the draw-

bridge got stuck. Rather than let you down, I swam across the
river (look, my suit's still damp), ran out to the airport, got a
hitch in Mr. Harriman's helicopter, landed on top of Radio City
Music Hall, and was carried here piggy-back by one of the
Rockettes." "You'll have to do better than that, Erskine," said the
boss, obviously disappointed. "No woman can get ready in ten
minutes."

Mrs. George Backer boasted to her Swopian Literary Circle
that her husband had given up smoking for a year. "That must
have taken plenty of self-control," said Arlene Francis admir-
ingly. "Exactly," agreed Mrs. Backer, "and that's just what I've
got."

The origin of the word "incompatibility" is perfectly clear to
Comedian Abe Burrows. "When a husband loses his income,"
points out Burrows, "you'll notice how promptly his wife loses
her patibility."

John Daly says he can prove that men are warmer than women.
Just consult a weather report. Doesn't it always read something
like, "Max. 82; Min. 34"?

When Pat O'Leary's wife presented him with his eleventh offspring in the space of thirteen years, the office force chipped in
to present him with a well-earned gift—a silver tray with what
they told him was the O'Leary coat of arms emblazoned thereon.
"What's the idea of putting that funny lookin' duck on me coat

of arms?" protested O'Leary. "That's no duck," explained the
office manager. "That's a stork with his legs worn off."

Mr. Honeyfuggler is looking for a new job. He lost his old one
when he thoughtlessly introduced his bird-brained bride to the
head of the firm at an office get-together. "So you're my Henry's
boss," gurgled Mrs. Honeyfuggler. "He's told me so much about
you, Mr. Legree!"

Charles Lee is showing friends a cartoon he clipped from an
English weekly. It depicts a couple of fellows playing darts in a
London saloon. One of the darts has gone out of line and clipped
a table sitter in the back of the noggin. The table sitter's girl
friend is impatiently grumbling, "Oh, you and your stabbing pains
in the head."

A publisher's wife told Irving Hoffman, "It's not true that I
married a millionaire. I made him one." "What was he before you
married him?" asked Irving. The wife answered, "A multi-million-
aire."

The president of the Wallager Falls bridge club enjoys showing off her young son's store of scientific knowledge to her fellow
members. One day she urged, "Go on and tell them, Jerome, what
it means when steam comes out of the spout of the kettle." "It
means," said Jerome, "that you are about to open one of Father's
letters."

The housekeeper of a crusty old bachelor was given to writing voluminous reports when her employer was away. As he left for a vacation he told her, "I want all the news, but for the love of heaven, be brief!" Four days later he received this note from her: "There has been a flood. Where your house was, the river is. Respectfully, Bridget Schinasi."

The new maid had been functioning, in a manner of speaking, for two weeks, and since she had shown no response to instruction, threats, or cajolery, Mrs. Brown decided to try sarcasm on her. "Do you know, Maymie," she said, "that man was created from dust?" "Yas'm," said Maymie. "And that when people die they turn back into dust?" "Yas'm," said Maymie. "Well," said Mrs. Brown forcefully, "I looked under the parlor rug this morning, Maymie, and there's quite a crowd there either coming or going!"

George Hcister tells of a tired businessman whose grueling day at the office was capped by his wife's announcement that the maid had walked out. "What was the trouble this time?" he inquired wearily. "*You* were!" she charged. "She said you used insulting language to her over the phone this morning." "Good grief," cried the husband. "I thought I was talking to you!"

Somerset Hemingwell sat happily typing the final pages of his new novel. In the yard, his nine-year-old son had just tripped over a tree root and broken his leg. The boxer puppy had chewed up Mrs. Hemingwell's best curtain, the twins had spilled a can of paint in the parlor and were now trying to pull each other's hair out, and the nurse had given notice. Mrs. Hemingwell paused in front of her husband's door and called out, "Lunch will be ready in a few moments. How far have you gotten with your manuscript?" Mr. H. answered, "It's going like a house-afire. The hero is just proposing to the heroine." "Give it a happy ending," begged Mrs. H. earnestly. "Have her say 'no'!"